The Bondage of Power: Learning to Hope

Michael Demkovich, OP

A Trilogy on Trust

Epilogue

DWP
Desert Willow Project

Cover design by M. Demkovich.
Photo *Die Macht zu Lande* fountain detail courtesy of https://commons.wikimedia.org

Demkovich, Michael

The Bondage of Power: Learning to Hope. A Trilogy on Trust: Learning to Love, Believe, and Hope Again.

ISBN 978-1-7345410-2-1

Spirituality. Catholic Philosophy. Theology. Self help

In a time of uncertainty, hostility, and mistrust, we have here a trilogy on ways of finding their opposite directions. Theologian Michael Demkovich has composed three short books to look at sources of conflict and mistrust in our modern times, as well as alternatives. He sees them unfolding from three thinkers called the "masters of suspicion:" the psychologist Sigmund Freud, the economist Karl Marx, and the philosopher Friedrich Nietzsche. This third book, *The Bondage of Power: Learning to Hope*, responds to Nietzsche's mistrust of the world, his proclamation of widespread unreality, and his philosophy of tensions between personal fulfillment and social reality. The alternative is hope.

These pages offer a journey through contemporary political and psychological issues with corresponding insights from contemporary spiritual writers. The conclusion offers "five faces" for a deeper life: benevolence, reliability, competence, honesty and openness. A succinct but rich volume on escaping the power of mistrust and finding hope as a dynamic of human life, as a gift of nature and of grace.

-Very Rev. Louis Morrone, O.P.
Prior Provincial, Dominican Province
St. Albert the Great (USA)

Hope is essential to a fulfilling life. Today's society is full of anxiety, polarization and loneliness. Instead of hope, we are riddled with suspicion and mistrust about the goodness of life, of people, and of relationships. Through his *Trilogy on Trust*, Michael Demkovich offers a practical guide to restoring our hope in the human community. This series takes on three "masters of suspicion" whose philosophical thoughts have contributed to the downfall of trust in society. "If we fail to ask why and how things influence us…" Demkovich tells us, "…we become easy dupes to be manipulated as the marketing industry knows so well."

This third book in his series, *The Bondage of Power: Learning to Hope*, examines the work of Friedrich Nietzsche. As a master of suspicion, Nietzsche's "campaign on morality" has eroded the very notion of values, of truth, and of the person in modern culture and left us tied up in a tangled noose of knots. Fr. Demkovich expertly unravels each complex knot and presents us with an alternative answer to Nietzsche's pessimism: hope – hope in ourselves, in society and in humanity. Fr. Demkovich has a genius for making complex philosophers such as Nietzsche, Marx and Freud accessible to every audience. Drawing upon well-known cultural references from film, art, music and daily life, *The Bondage of Power: Learning to Hope* is a truly enjoyable and deeply compelling read, and something that is dearly needed in our world today.

-Anastasia Wendlinder, Ph.D.,
Associate Professor of Religious Studies,
Gonzaga University

Table of Contents

Preface.. .1
1. Introduction: Razzle Dazzle World..................... 6
2. The Power Problem: "I Think I Can"...14
3. A Tangled Noose of Knots...............................21
4. The First Knot: *"Must we ourselves become gods?"*..25
5. The Second Knot: *"Pursue what is forbidden. There is no truth."*..31
6. The Third Knot: *The Will to Power. The Power to Control*..35
7. The Fourth Knot: *Master-Slave. Beyond Good and Evil*..45
8. The Fifth Knot: *The Joy of Destruction*...............51
9. The Sixth Knot: *"I know my destiny; I am the Annihilator."*...56
10. The Art of Untying Knots: De-Con-struction.......61
11. The Beauty of Bondage...................................64
12. Hope Beyond Hope: Pandora and the Dumb Ox....69
13. Conclusion, From Suspicion to Trust.................78
An Epilogue to *A Trilogy on Trust*.......................83
Brief Bibliography..88
Acknowledgments...90

Preface

I am aware, that for some readers, this present work is your first book in *The Trilogy on Trust*. So, it will be helpful to know what this book and the other two are aiming to do. All three books are taking a look at trust, and in particular, the philosophical influences that seem to undermine trust and create suspicion. When I began this project, it was pre-COVID and the mistrust was largely political. However, over time it has become pervasive. In the last century or more, three prominent philosophers have increasingly and significantly impacted our thinking. Whether we realize it or not, whether it is obvious or not, their influence is critical. These three thinkers have been called "the masters of suspicion," and they are the psychologist Sigmund Freud, the economist Karl Marx, and the philosopher Friedrich Nietzsche. If we fail to ask why and how things influence us, we become easy dupes to be manipulated as the marketing industry knows so well. It was Socrates who said "The unexamined life is not worth living." Whereas modern day "influencers" seem to say "don't bother, I will tell you what to think."

The Tyranny of Perfection: Finding True Pleasure, was the first work wherein we examined the false notion that things must be and have to be perfect. It is our suspicion when people don't meet our high standards that undermine trust. The basis of all gossip is to undermine a person's reputation, to influence individual interaction negatively with that person, who is the object of our gossip. In each of these books, I have surveyed the obstacles each philosophy places upon our trust and have offered one of the great virtues, also called theological virtues, to present a counterpoint against the mistrust. In the first book, it was the virtue of love. Our ability to see the good even in the brokenness of life. Love is not deterred by the imperfect but enters into the reality of life itself. The second book, *The Want of Wealth: Discovering Real Worth*, treated the impact of Marxist mistrust generated by our monetization of life and human greed. When we reduce a person's worth to their monetary wealth, it is the virtue of Faith, our openness to believe in the other, that restores their true value, found not in money but in their meaning. Both Freud and Marx cast suspicion on our inter-personal dynamics, that is reality outside a person - some ideal norm of perfection and an economic class-based order. What we will see in this work is Nietzsche's mistrust of reality itself, the individual's rebellion against the world in order to create one's own reality, or illusion of it. This is an isolating and alienating stance. One that sees personal power over the other as the standard of authentic living.

I confess, exploring Nietzsche has been a challenge to appreciate his thought and how he has been used or misused after his death. In part, the challenge is found in his own evolution in thought. He only lived to be 56 and as he aged, his health declined, he abandoned university teaching, was unrequited in love by Lou Salomé, and eventually ended up somewhat isolated. If one reads his early works, prior to *The Dawn of Day* (1881), you're given the impression of a novel thinker and a critical questioner of the *status quo*. This is what many young university students find attractive, even today. However, his mature writings grew out of greater isolation, what he called his "campaign against morality."[1] He sought to undo the very notion of values, of truth, and of the person. Interpreting his thought is further compounded by the efforts of his sister and by the subsequent misuse of his thoughts by fascists and National Socialists. Even with these various layers at play, it is important to recognize Nietzsche's influence on our world today.

We have all had the experience of a string, a shoelace, even the garden hose getting tangled into a knot. Sometimes the knot is so tightly made that it is almost impossible to untie. Knots have provided me with a metaphor for appreciating Nietzsche's complicated and intricate ideas. It is a way for us to look at his ideas and their impact. After each knot I provide a simple, brief question meant to help us better appreciate the impact of his thought. In addition, it will be beneficial if I offer a comment on two terms we will encounter — "power" and "relations." As I began this trilogy on trust, it was clear that suspicion and mistrust employed the realities of sex, money, and power as corrosive, causing one to doubt reality. By that, I mean the division created when we reduce the moral action of those with whom we disagree

---

[1]Friedrich Nietzsche *Ecce Homo: How One Becomes What One Is* Anthony Ludovici trans (Anados Book 2019 first published 1911) p. 41. In this work Nietzsche offers his understanding of almost of his writings where he uses this phrase to describe his work, *The Dawn of Days*.

merely to be motivated by salacious, financial, and/or imperious gains. In the previous two works we have seen the tyranny of an oppressive puritanism that undermines self-acceptance and personal maturity, as well as the monetization of social life. Now we explore the distorted notion of autocratic power.

Consequently, we need to ask "What do we mean by power?" This will be developed in the subsequent chapters, but a distinction to keep in mind from the get-go is our use of power as a moral question. Power always holds the potential for good but also for evil. Power is about the potential or possibility to achieve an end. However, power may be abused as coercive, controlling, and destructive. On the one hand, power in its best sense is moral and is ordered to the good. Identifying and achieving the good requires a broader framework than one's individual view, one's private truth. Isolation and alienation are foreign to human flourishing and the most destructive weapon in the political arsenal. Us-Them thinking is behind all war, genocide and persecution since Cane killed his brother Abel.

It is the notion of relation that compels us to ask questions beyond just the one thing (*a res*) and that of something other (*alius*). This is important because relation is reality (*res aliter*) as the Latin roots of these words show. Being real is being related, engaging, time and time again, the other, for each thing is enriched by the other. Corrupted power or malicious authority must be challenged. Oppression takes many forms and the abuse of power can have many allies. Here is where power can be mishandled and it alienates even those who claim to be "in power." I contend that it is the virtue of hope, something Nietzsche denies along with all the Christian virtues, that places us outside of our self and in relationship to others. A person who hopes sees the redemptive importance of relationships. We need one another to find happiness. I know that the world of ideas and philosophical language seems strange to many, but unless we explore, ask questions, challenge our assumptions and go deeper, we are held captive to the bondage of power.

Chapter 1.

Introduction: Razzle Dazzle World

I wonder why power is such a significant thing. Who really possesses power? How is power meant to be used? Is power's bondage only of others or does power hold captive its agents? When I was younger, teaching morality to college students, I remember it was during the height of the Cold War. The arms race with Russia and the United States, both seeking a "balance of power." In one of my classes I made the comment "peace through armament is terrorism." It was a catchy phrase to lure my students into the debate. One student liked it and made a bumper sticker out of it to challenge the war hawks. In those days it drew comment from both sides. However, it failed to realize what was the more important issue, which I should have realized given the context of contemporary Christian morality. That issue was our need to address the very reason for armament, or the arms race. That reason simply put is the issue of trust, or more correctly mistrust, humanity's ruptured relationships. Relationality and relationships are critical to life that engages the world. Without relations we simply live in isolations. Idiots in the truest sense of the Greek meaning isolated, private, just me (ἰδιώτης).

President Reagan had a very important insight on building trust. Trust requires moral inter-action on the part of both parties involved. "Trust, but verify" is an important way to build peace and trust through moral action. It seems to me now that the fundamental issue of mistrust is our lost sense of a common humanity. But why is that?

I think one way to make sense of this question of trust can be found in the thought of a French philosopher named Rene Girard. A concept of his that has stayed with me is known as "scapegoating." We may be familiar with the phrase "to be a scapegoat," and we may even be familiar with its origins in Levitical law. But to ask the philosophical question of human mistrust and violence, as Girard does, moves the concept to its purpose and focuses us on our using not goats but other humans as our "scapegoats." In Leviticus, it was humanity's religious way of making a sacrifice to God in order to restore our relationships through forgiveness and a deepening of our humanity. Religion and religious mindedness are an important meta-language for human flourishing. And our great failure has been to dismiss it, remove it from our common lexicon. In the second book of this trilogy, I spoke of the "golden braid" which links together religion, science, and art: the good, the true, and the beautiful. This golden braid enables us as humans to transcend and behold a larger vision of life itself.

Blaming is nothing new, and it is the surest tactic of many young children who have yet to learn moral responsibility. It is much easier to blame someone else and fail to engage a larger understanding. This phrase, "a larger understanding" holds us to the task of exploring big ideas, going beyond the superficial. In all three of these books, I have engaged the larger understandings of several philosophers, Freud, Marx, and Nietzsche. If we fail to think bigger, to pursue a larger understanding, we abandon one of the unique characteristics of humanity, and that is our love of wisdom. It is so much easier to blame. I am amazed at how easy it is for me to do so when my favorite sports team loses its game. I blame the other team, I blame the referees, I blame everyone else, but normally not my own team. I may blame a particular player on my team, and may even sympathetically explain their failure. But otherwise, I know beyond the shadow of a doubt that some idiot, who is blind as a bat, who is biased in favor of the other team, and who should lose his or her job is at fault. I even dislike the other team more and over the years I grow in hatred for them and anyone who supports them. Now, at face value, we can see the juvenile, immature, and biased thinking that believes this is true. It's only when I pursue a larger understanding that I realize none of those reasons are realistic. In sports, let's say in football, we can have very intense and strong feelings, but if we do not engage the larger questions, we fail to make use of our human ability to think, to understand, and to know. We grow less human. I think this is important, because it has become more and more the reality of our world today, we are becoming less human. [By the way, according to GOOGLE the Dallas Cowboys were the most disliked NFL team as of January 2023.]

When I began to work on the *Tyranny of Perfection*, the first in this trilogy, it was pre-Covid amid the political efforts of the Democrats to impeach the president. Division was a constant anthem of the nation. Politicians sought to harness their power following Saul Alinsky's rules for radicals to isolate, ridicule, and embarrass. Impeach, impeach, impeach was the slogan and I witnessed, with great embarrassment, the failure of American political life, our increasing de-humanization. We have lost the ability to engage in reasonable discussion and rational argument. The great national debate has given way to organized protest by those promoting a rhetoric of hate. We have lost any philosophical critical self-reflection. In an effort to claim moral legitimacy we create a self-serving narrative, a fiction that has replaced fact -- rational thought was replaced by a well told narrative, rehearsed and repeated by our preferred media outlet. Network television and social media are labeled as "credible sources" not based on truth, but on likes. We find that a lie told often enough becomes believable. The Y2K malaise created a postmodern mistrust of the reasonable, dismissing and ignoring the standards of classical thought. "Out with the old and in with the new" is the fool's slogan of every radical revolutionary. The false notion of modern progress was criticized for its Enlightenment failures which crumbled under its own shifting sands. Now, if you are bewildered and questioning my state of mind, you very likely have been educated since the American cultural revolution of the 1960s and that is troubling. Let me explain.

Over decades of teaching, I have come to recognize that look of growing disinterest. As Americans, we like the simple, pragmatic explanation assuming that all reality is easily captured in bite-size pieces, K.I.S.S. ("keep it simple stupid"). For most of us we are content with the *Crayola 8 Pack*, we function, and are happy with the basics. However, some realities require more colors, more options, more clarification. The *Crayola 96 Pack* certainly delivers. While my coloring book, or my worldview, can get by with brown, pink, orange, yellow, green, blue, purple, and black, I must face the fact that there are more colors, there is a bigger picture, a larger vision. In Philosophy we examine the colors and pigment of human imagination and ultimate meaning. The philosophical task is to try to understand, in full color, and we face an honest critique of our ideas and their relationship to things. Marx, Freud, and Nietzsche have tried to convince us that we don't need to bother with the nuances of life. All can be reduced to pleasure, wealth, and power. We end up, living in the shadows of lies, innuendos, and suggestions, because we have denied truth, morality, and integrity.

The 1975 musical based on Maurine Dallas Watkins' 1926 play titled "Chicago" was based on the true story of two criminals Beulah Annan and Belva Gartner, in the Cook County jail for murder, and who were both acquitted. It was made into a comedy called "Roxie Hart" in 1942. The story shows us a twisted moral order wherein the criminal is celebrated by the media and the justice system corrupted and manipulated. The concept of justice or law is nullified by a bribe-taking warden, a dishonest lawyer, and a sensationalist media that promotes a false razzle dazzle narrative. It was revived on Broadway in 1996 in the wake of the O.J. Simpson courtroom drama and media spectacle. This Tony winning musical promotes the false narrative of celebrity criminals Velma Kelly and Roxie Hart. We see that the false became the real in a masterful number "We both reached for the gun" sung during the "Press Conference Rag." The media, manipulated by a corrupt, slick lawyer believes the lie Roxie tells to be true. It is a fable of our modern mistrust, justified one might say, given the world today. Biased media, corrupted legal political systems, bought public opinion, and social media distorting ("influencing") what is the really real. The most genuine character, Roxie's husband, goes unnoticed and dismissed as 'Mr. Cellophane.' The theater is a safe place to look at life, to challenge and comment on culture, and on Broadway "Chicago" did just that. The ancient Greeks celebrated dramas over 2500 years ago.[2] The Colosseum in Rome entertained with battles and executions. Elizabethan England produced a rich theater heritage

---

[2] For the Greeks theater was part of the Dionysian, a way to address the dark side of our humanity. What we will see is that Nietzsche failed to look beyond, focusing chiefly on the Greek tragedy, interpreting Greek culture too narrowly. For the Greeks, the amphitheater was the place for communal celebration of the tragic (good people at odds through no fault to their own), the comic (the juxtaposition of incongruous ideas), and the erotic (the satire, who was half man and half beast, in the state of arousal). Modern day theater embodies all three in our collective appreciation of the dark and light, the Dionysian and the Apollonian, even the symbol for the theater are the masks of comedy and tragedy. Theater, even to this day, serves to connect humanity. The stage is where we can share the drama of humanity. However, the stage is not reality even though it is real.

thriving today in London and Broadway and elsewhere. Even Hollywood has impacted our social consciousness. However, they may reflect reality, but they fall short of the complexity of things. *Chicago* helps us to see the dirty secret of corruption and moral bankruptcy.

This book, *The Bondage of Power* explores the underlying distortion that has brought us to the political maneuvering which alienates our common life and de-humanizes us all. In this trilogy, we have shown how the late 20th Century's turn toward interpretation and away from examination, toward opinion and away from analysis, have placed us in a world of doubt. Sex, pleasure, money, and power contribute to the landscape, but they are not the whole of our reality. The real world, the true measure of things, depends upon complex and inter-relational dynamics. The bondage I wish to address is the stagnant imposition of force or power to control, limit and divide. This has been fed by a philosophy found in the German thinker, Friedrich Nietzsche (1844–1900). During his life, his influence was limited, but after the two world wars and the existential question of meaning, he has emerged as an influential voice to the post 1960s cultural revolutionaries. The chronic tendency to tear down with the naïve promise that something better is bound to emerge is key to his thought. The adolescent notion to run away rather than to engage, to make believe rather than to believe, is his craft. Nietzsche's influence upon the postmodern thinkers, the deconstructionist thought of Jean François Lyotard, Jacques Derrida; and the post structuralism of William S. Burrow have impacted ethnic and race theories of privilege and punishment, repeating the racial superiority tragically manifested in the Nazi extermination of the unfit, the weak, the queer, the Jew. What we call the radical left progressivism is strongly directed by the thought of "French Nietzscheanism" in writers like Michelle Foucault (1926–1984) and others. We are like coal miners, who are unaware of the toxic impact of ideology. Lacking the canary to sound an alarm we breath these toxic ideologies unknowingly. The deliberate dismantling of classical education has removed philosophical inquiry, creating a toxic atmosphere that de-humanizes and impacts our quality of life. Ideology versus reality, what I think it is versus what it is, has given us the razzle dazzle world. In order to free oneself from the bondage of power, we must rightly know the bonds that hold us back. As with the other two works, I examine here the last of the Masters of Suspicion, Friedrich Nietzsche and the question of power. How it is this power can tie and tether us in the many knots of Nietzsche's colorless world. While power to control moves us toward alienation and isolation we see that our interconnectedness, our common bond, which Nietzsche misses, compels us to hope, which offers us real power.

Chapter 2.

The Power Problem: "I Think I Can"

"I think I can - I think I can - I think I can" these simple words from the children's story of the *The Little Engine that Could* demonstrate the issue of power: what we might do, what we can do, what we could do, and what we should do. In this trilogy on trust, the role of Friedrich Nietzsche, the 19th century philosopher, is one of the more challenging "Masters of Suspicion" for us to understand. In the previous works Sigmund Freud's role in a false world of perfection and Karl Marx's role monetizing human worth were clear, but Nietzsche's role in understanding power is more complicated. Complicated because his thought is more challenging and at the same time more appealing to us. We have an ambivalence concerning a philosophy of "might makes right." It repulses us when used unjustly and compels us when we are in need of true justice. Nietzsche articulated an alternate ethical order wherein the individual creates his or her own system of values. Consequently, each person challenges every assumption made as to its moral purpose and goal. While both Freud and Marx mistrusted our relation to things outside ourselves, Nietzsche's mistrust is of the world's relationship to us, questioning the value of existing principles that guide our lives, that nestle us into some natural order of things, he insists that we make values that are our own individual creation, which we impose upon the world and others.

But what do we mean by value? In one sense it is

arbitrary and subjective. If there doesn't exist an absolute against which we judge things then all is questionable. For example, in *The Want of Wealth* we saw that the value of the U.S. Dollar is no longer set against a gold standard, rather its so-called value is derived from other currencies, the U.S. Treasury's interest on notes, and on dollars held in foreign governments. To speak of the thing's value is not something intrinsic or innate like gold, but now it is seen as relative. So how can we determine the value of anything?

In the work *The Will to Power*[3] we find the context of thinking for Nietzsche, which was a world of nihilism, that all values are baseless and that nothing can be known. He had written "nihilism is at our door" describing it as "the absolute repudiation of worth, purpose, and desirability." In his disdain for religion, he finds the fault for nihilism in Christianity, stating "nihilism harbors in the hearts of Christian morals."[4] It is an attractive premise to blame Christianity for deceiving some societies. In the same citation he earlier wrote, "the highest values are long losing their value." What makes Nietzsche's thought so appealing is its ambiguity that shifts morality from objective standards to subjective

---

[3] This work is one of Nietzsche's unpublished manuscripts that his sister Elizabeth Forrester Nietzsche likely edited for her own agenda. The common belief is that his sister's anti-Semitic, pro-Nazi ideology impacted the edited works after her brother's death. For example, David Wroe *"'Criminal' manipulation of Nietzsche by sister to make him look anti-Semitic"*. The Daily Telegraph (19 January 2010).

[4] *Will to Power*. Book 1

ones. Reality is mistrusted and one's own conception of value replaces reality itself. In other words, reality comes about as a consequence of our concepts, rather than the mind's deriving its concepts from reality. The adolescent appeal of creating a new world is attractive to every idealist in history and every radical revolutionary.

As mentioned, there is the children's story about a little engine that must pull a long train over a steep terrain. All the bigger, more powerful engines were asked to pull the train, but they all refused to do so. Only the little engine took up the task. As he struggled to pull the heavy cars up the steep hill, he kept saying to himself, "I think I can, I think I can, I think I can." Power, we see, is about making real, it is about actualizing what is potential. It is a creative act. The little train didn't know if he could, nor if he should do it, but something made him try. His encouraging slogan holds key notions that demonstrate the challenge of power which we need to explore. "**I**" is the "who" or agent of power. "**Think**" is the potential, the "what" that is possible of power. And "**Can**" is the "how" or the conviction to do, the actualizing or realized power. However, here we find an interesting word "can" because in its etymology, its root meaning, we see that it is also a kind of knowledge. It differs from thinking about ideas in that it is a practical, applied knowledge, the "know how to do" of power. Now these three elements are fundamental aspects of power, its cause or it's making things to be.

Even a simple story can teach us important philosophical ideas. The Greek philosopher Aristotle spoke of four causes, which he described as the formal cause which is the initiating cause, like "I need a table for my dining room." A material cause like "I bought some mahogany for making this table." An efficient cause like my working every day to make the table. And lastly a final cause like dining with my friends at the table I made. These causes of power are helpful for us to appreciate Nietzsche's philosophy. The little engine's slogan "I think I can" relies on the subject, the "I" as the material cause (the "stuff" to be acted upon) and also the formal cause (the "thinking" or idea of what is to be achieved). The efficient cause is found in the desired goal conceived in my thinking (the "can"). Unlike the mahogany in my example the "stuff" is the individual person, the subject. But this subject is also the formal ideal of what "I" want to end up with, and it is the subject or "I" that must do the work. This empowering role of the individual subject as one's desire to realize a thing and one's will to actually achieve a thing, this is the basic point of the story. The little engine is a story of believing in one's self in order to achieve greatness. A good lesson indeed, but it is missing something. What is missing from the engine's slogan is the final cause, the "why" which we assume is to get the entire train itself up the hill. But what if the goal were something else? Pride or riches or control? What if the engine did it to show he was better than all the other engines? What if he did it because he thought he would get a big reward from the company whose goods he transported up the hill? What if he did it to confiscate and control the goods and resources in its cargo? "Why" is the question word of value. It is the final cause of moral worth and meaning. Values are the fundamental issue behind every why, the ultimate cause of human action.

This issue of values is key to human flourishing, for it holds what is good and right. We find in one of Nietzsche's works, *The Antichrist*[5] (1888) his raising fundamental questions that recast values in terms of power. He proclaims:

> What is good? – Whatever augments the feeling of power, the will to power, power itself in man. What is evil? – Whatever springs from weakness. What is happiness? – The feeling that power increases -- that resistance is overcome. Not contentment, but more power; not peace at any price, but war; not virtue, but efficiency (virtue in the Renaissance sense, *virtu*, virtue free of moral acid). The weak and the botched shall perish: first principle of our charity. And one should help them to it. What is more harmful than any vice? – Practical sympathy for the botched and the weak – Christianity... (*The Antichrist*, p. 18)

Once value is recast in terms of power for power, and pleasure for pleasure, it is difficult to find the truly trustworthy outside of one's own pleasure garden of power. To illustrate this, in the 2017 Marvel Cinematic Universe movie *Thor: Ragnarök* we find the difference between power for power and true power. Hela (played

---

[5] *The Antichrist*. H.L.Mencken trans. & Introduction. Tribeca Books, 2010.

by Cate Blanchett) and Thor (played by Chris Hemsworth) embody the issue of power. Hela is out to destroy and enslave the weak as would Nietzsche. She loathes the weakness of the aged Odin, of her sibling Thor, and of all who are "botched and weak." Her power is without true value apart from a self-serving power for power. Thor, on the other hand, shows us another kind of power, a power whose purpose is the right, the good and the just. Unlike Hela, whose power is drawn from spreading her realm acquiring more and more control, more power, more destruction, Thor's power come from within. The moral power is captured in Odin's words to his son, "Asgaard is not a place. Never was …Asgaard is where our people stand."

In order to understand Nietzsche, we have to wade through his sometimes seeming to be contradictions, the use and abuse of his ideas for political ends, and the various efforts of scholars to re-interpret him.[6] Not only in the reception of his thought, but in the provocative reactions that his works generate, that we are bewitched. To be a philosopher today seems an unlikely career, yet Nietzsche's trade was that of ideas and the crafting of social thought. Most people today are a bit bored by the philosophical, but the big questions of life and human existence are timeless. They must be answered rightly, which is the task of philosophy. Consequently, I wish to take a closer look at Nietzsche's concepts as a tangled noose of knots.

[6] Walter Kaufman, Bernard Reginster, Paul Katsafanas, Christine Korsgaard, David Velleman, Brian Leiter, to name a few.

Chapter 3.

A Tangled Noose of Knots

Nietzsche's significance ought not to be dismissed, he embodies the post-modern struggle of life's meaninglessness. His own life is indicative of our world's sense of hopelessness and despair. In order to appreciate his role in the bondage of power a brief look at the cultural climate of the 19th century Europe will help. As we saw with both Sigmund Freud (1856-1939) and Karl Marx (1818-1883), their Age's social and political change shaped them and their mistrust of pleasure and economics. It is clear that the 19th century was marked by industrialization, capitalism, materialism, and individualism. The challenge of the Age was political, the role and relation of the individual and society – how people were to relate, as a whole and as parts. Sigmund Freud brought attention to the inner person and one's psychological well-being. Karl Marx brought attention to the economic forces dominating social interaction. Both men reasonably looked to causes in the world, in one's environment. However, with Freidrich Nietzsche the shift is to the inner world of one's own subjective making. For him the question was an individual's coping with the chaos, and making for one's self a "higher man."

For the young Nietzsche, his situation was significantly altered when at the age of five, he lost both his father and his younger and only brother, when both died unexpectedly. He grew up with his mother, Franziska and sister Elisabeth, in the home of his maternal grandmother in Naumburg. He studied to be a Lutheran minister and excelled in the study of Greek, but he abandoned theology and religion to focus on philosophy as he understood it. For him philosophy ought to have the pragmatic end of bringing about a better world, similar to Marx' view. His famous statement about religion in Europe was "God is dead. God remains dead. And we have killed him" (*The Gay Science*) which captures his world. This "loss" collapsed all of the institutions and assumptions that gave foundational meaning, leaving only the rubble of doubt and mistrust. In other words, his world ended, and it confronted him with the need to redefine the world he wanted. While Karl Marx had criticized religion as the "opiate of the people," distracting people from the oppressive structures, Nietzsche replaced religion with self-empowerment. His critique ultimately brings him to deny truth itself. Now, in order to help us understand his meaning, I suggest we see that Nietzsche began tying knots. Here we sense the bondage of power not only over others, but over one's self as well. To keep himself from sinking into nihilism and from drifting off into the myth of religion, he needed to moor himself, so to say, by knotting himself to the self. The knots were tied by him with each doubt and uncertainty.

If God is dead, then I need to replace God. Who best to do the job than me, so I must now provide what God once was able to provide. **KNOT 1**: *I must necessarily be and become God*. However, without some absolute reality beyond myself there can't be some universal truth that all people are obligated to accept. **KNOT 2**: *There is no truth, there are only various perspectives.* Consequently, without the surety of God and absolute truth, the undeniable affirmation is one's own feeling of power. **KNOT 3:** *Power, my power, is my only concern.* With power as one's motive or reason for being, a person's goal is to be the master and to dominate the weak. **KNOT 4:** *You are either a master or a slave.* As a master, your happiness derives from the power you possess. Power to inflict pain and to experience pleasure. **KNOT 5:** *Pleasure is life affirming.* Artist and art-making, these are life affirming acts which offer a person beauty, the illusion of living well. The artistry of one's life is found in creating one's character. **Knot 6:** *Craft your character so as to appear beautiful.* As one creates one's self as a beautiful individual, not enslaved by society, religion, morality, the independent individual finds freedom, in other words, be a free spirit, do not follow the herd.

The problem with knots is that they tie things and in fact restrict things and limit a person. Even though Nietzsche understood this as producing, if only fleetingly, a glimpse of his "over man" (*die Übermensch*), the highest man, or the superman, we see that what results is self-loathing, self-alienation and isolation. The danger of being an absolute divine, of one's own making, is that the social aspect of human flourishing is lost. The 2017 Marvel film *The Guardians of the Galaxy* has a character who captures this knot of Nietzsche that can tie and limit a person. In the aptly named character Ego (Kurt Russell), who is a god-like celestial, we discover he is the father of the main character, Peter Quill (Chris Pratt). Ego creates, out of his consciousness his world, the world he wants. His sole goal is to transform thousands of worlds into himself by destroying what is not like him in order for it to be him. Even the planet where he lives is made of his own creation, in fact it is him. Ego draws power from the transformation of worlds into himself or more precisely by their destruction. Here is a bit of a twist, Quill's mother, Meredith, whom Ego says he genuinely loved, and for whom Quill has great love, breaks the spell Ego held over his son by a simple truth. Ego accidentally discloses that he had to destroy even the one he claims to have loved. Ego confesses in front of Quill, saying "it broke my heart to put that tumor in her head." This truth awakens in Quill his awareness of the destructive design of Ego that not only destroyed his mother, but would inevitably destroy even his friends. Here we can see the destructive knot of a self-centered acquisition of pleasure and power. It is a black hole that destroys even the ability to love by destroying the very object of love – the other.

The bondage of power is this consumptive need for more power that insulates one's self from what is in fact, the greatest form of power, and that is empowerment, the empowering relationship of the other – in a word love. In the following chapters we will explore, these knots and there restrictive and destructive role in the fuller understanding of power.

Chapter 4

The First Knot: *"Must we ourselves become gods?"*

In Nietzsche's guide to becoming "what one is," which was first published in 1908 as *Ecce Homo* [EH], he gives his evaluation of many of his major works. It provides a helpful tool for us to treat his works and thought, given our limited space. But more so, as it is his own assessment of these works, we hear his own understanding of his *corpus*.

The *Birth of Tragedy* (1872) is one of Nietzsche's earliest works where we see the dilemma between chaos and order. Given his fascination for ancient Greek culture he characterizes this tension as Dionysian (the negation of things) and Apollonian (the affirmation of things). It is the dichotomy of darkness/light, disorder/order, which is a necessary conflict for Nietzsche who writes, "an idea – the antagonism of the two concepts, Dionysian and Apollonian – is translated into metaphysics; history itself is depicted as the development of this idea in tragedy. This antithesis has become unity; from this standpoint things which therefore had never been face to face are suddenly confronted, and understood, and illumined by each other…." (EH 31). It is this newfound awareness of the Dionysian impulse taken as "a yea-saying attitude to life" (*ibid.*) that he sees as liberating, a "yea-saying free from all reserve, applying even to suffering, and guilt, and all that is questionable and strange in existence" (EH 32).

Once a person is freed from idealism, from thinking there is an order to things, one is able to soar "above the pitiful foolish gabble" (EH 32). Nietzsche assumes he is the first to discover the value of exposing this self-deception. In Biblical stories the wayward soul is well documented. But Nietzsche, in a naïve exuberance declares: "I was the first to see the actual contrast: the degenerate instinct which turns upon life with a subterranean lust of vengeance (Christianity…in short, the whole of idealism in its typical forms), as opposed to formula of the highest yea-saying to life, born of an abundance and a superabundance of life – a yea-saying free from all reserve, applying even to suffering, and guilt, and all that is questionable and strange in existence" (EH 32). Once you set aside an ultimate Edenic moral order you are let loose in a garden of personal pleasure and delight. It is the fantasy of every adolescent (no matter one's age) to be free of parental guidance, to get the keys to the car, or to have the house to yourself for a weekend. Nietzsche continues: "This last, most joyous, most exuberant and exulted yea to life, is not only the highest, but also the profoundest conception, and one which is most strictly confirmed, and supported by truth and science. Nothing that exists must be suppressed, and nothing can be dispensed with. These aspects of life which Christians and other Nihilist reject, belongs to an incalculably higher order in the hierarchy of values, than that which the instinct of degeneration calls good, and may call good" (*ibid.*). For Nietzsche it is this rejection of anything considered taboo or wrong and as being just as valuable as all that is endorsed by society and labelled as good. Today we see it in the question of gender identity or the rejection of biological distinctions. Nietzsche sees Christianity as a barrier to a fulsome embrace of existence, the good and the bad. He explains:

> …In order to understand this, a certain courage is necessary, and, as a prerequisite of this, a certain superfluity of strength: for a man can approach only as near to truth, as he has the courage to advance – that is to say everything depends strictly upon the measure of his strength. Knowledge, and the affirmation of reality, are just as necessary to the strong man as cowardice and flight from reality – in fact, the "ideal"– are necessary to the weak inspired by weakness…. These people are not at liberty to "know" – decadents stand in need of lies, – it is one of their self-preservative measures. He, who not only understands the word "Dionysian," but understands *himself* in that term, does not require any refutation of Plato, or of Christianity, or of Schopenhauer – for his nose *scents decomposition* [sic.] (EH 32).

We may lie even about our own body in order to oppose the reality, sex changes, men self-defining as women. Nietzsche deplores the weakness of those who cannot reject the existing cultural values. It takes a certain strength to embrace the dark Dionysian side of reality, but for Nietzsche this is the great affirmation of life in all its dimensions. Think about it for a moment. Our current climate of anti-everything is the world Nietzsche offers and which rejects even reality itself.

To put Nietzsche in a nutshell, his fundamental start is to deny the traditional values of Christianity and of German culture (as he understood it in 19th century Germany). In a sense, such a critique of the established order is both exciting and angst ridden. It is a common dynamic and a good example of this "adolescent spirit" let loose of parental discipline as seen in the 1954 award winning novel by William Golding, *The Lord of the Flies*. It is a classic presentation of the devolution from order to chaos as adolescent boys, marooned on a primitive uninhabited island, turn from the ordered ideal view of Ralph (or the Apollonian view to use Nietzsche's concepts) and instead turning to the Dionysian view of Jack, who promises to hunt and destroy the imagined beast. Eventually, Jack and his band of boys seek to kill Ralph. In a clever parallel Golding shows us, this inhumanity of these boys, in the context of a nuclear war that threatens humanity itself. A pilot, who had parachuted out ends up dead hanging from a tree in the forest, which magnifies the boys' fears of the beast. In their frenzy to destroy Ralph (Apollonian order) Jack and the boys set fire to the forest, destroying their world. Ralph fleeing the fire and his hunters, trips and falls at the feet of a British naval officer. It is the return of a higher power and a moral order (the Apollonian order) which confronts all the boys with their Dionysian destructive actions, and they erupt into sobs of remorse. In a real way it is the loss of the absolute notion of good characterized in Jack's strong will and egomaniacal pursuit of power and violence that are the Dionysian world of Nietzsche. Fear of the "beast" is Jack's power over the boys. It is the lie of the beast, a false fear, that gives Jack power, mastery over the weak "choir boys" who abandon their religious self-awareness for primitive savagery. But, according to Nietzsche, it is the loss of the Apollonian that freed these boys in Jack's band from slavery of ideals to a world without God, a world of one's own making. Nietzsche would have deplored Golding's ending with its return to the Apollonian values as contrary to his understanding of yea-saying to life.

This theme, or knot, of one's turn to the Dionysian, is a rejection of the absolute and ultimate reality of the Christian and the God of Christianity, in Nietzsche's day. In his 1882 work, *The Gay Science* (also translated *The Joy for Wisdom*) this knot is most tightly made when Nietzsche declares several times his infamous quote. It is most clearly stated by the madman who declares: "God is dead. God remains dead. And we have killed him. How shall we comfort ourselves, the murderers of all murderers? What was holiest and mightiest of all that the world has yet owned has bled to death under our knives: who will wipe this blood off of us? What water is there for us to clean ourselves? What festivals of atonement, what sacred games shall we have to invent? Is not the greatness of this deed too great for us? Must we ourselves become gods simply to appear worthy of it?" (GS, section 125 Walter Kaufman translation).

Question 1: What value does the Apollonian bring and what kind of world are we left with void of the Absolute?

Chapter 5

The Second Knot: *"Pursue what is forbidden. There is no truth."*

A consequence of the death of God or loss of the absolute, is that the notion of Truth as an absolute is abandoned. For Nietzsche there is no Truth in the classical sense, but nothing more than various perspectives. Truth no longer defines us, but we now define truth. The 1883 story by Carlo Callodi recounts the puppet maker, Geppetto who so wanted a son that he created a boy puppet named *Pinocchio*. Even the puppet wished to be real. His dream to become a boy was granted by the Blue Fairy, but he must first prove himself to be brave, truthful, and unselfish. He is guided by Jiminy Cricket who serves as his conscience amid various challenges and temptations. One thing though, the puppet's nose would grow whenever he told a lie. The story shows the importance of truth in life. But why is truth telling or not lying so important? It is one of the primary lessons every child is taught, and we assume that "honesty is the best policy" as Sir Edwin Sandy held (a saying widely attributed to Benjamin Franklin). Even this pithy saying on honesty has an uncertain or questionable origin. However, for Nietzsche truth telling or not lying has a very different meaning. For him "honesty is the final virtue," but it is an honesty only to the yea-saying of one's own life. In a word, it is being honest or brave enough to pursue what is even forbidden. Ovid's maxim found in his *Amores* (III. 4:17) "*Nitimur in vetitum*" (which means: *pursue what is forbidden*) is the guiding principle of Nietzsche's thinking. He declares "…for that which has hitherto been most stringently forbidden, is without exception, Truth" (EH, 2). Let me repeat that: **"…for that which has hitherto been most stringently forbidden, is without exception, Truth."** Today the media and so-called news outlets pander the lie as true. Even academics of our highest institution avoid truth and reduce the question to context. Again, returning to the 1940 Disney's classic *Pinocchio*, the moral voice of Jiminy Cricket for Nietzsche would be replaced by the Disney character J. Worthington Foulfellow (a.k.a Honest John), whose name is a lie. He is a hedonist in the pursuit of self-pleasure and gain. So why is honesty, in a true sense important?

Nietzsche sees truth as being self-defined -- me being the one I choose to be. For him, it is the courage to be different, that is truth. Here we see the knotted-ness of this thinking. If truth is only what I have the guts to say is true, regardless of what reason and reality present, then there is no common ground. Nietzsche had a fascination for language as a philologist, his mind wrestled with language, and in his 1873 work *On Truth and Lies in a Non-Moral Sense* he presents his understanding. If truth is nothing more than a linguistic construct, then lies can be true, and the truth can be lies. I realize this sounds fantastic, but isn't it exactly where our political and legal institutions have come to? For Nietzsche "… truths are illusions, about which one has forgotten, that this is what they are; metaphors, which are worn out, and without serious, sensuous power; coins which have lost their pictures, and now matter only as metal, no longer as coins."[7]

"Pursuing what is forbidden" may seem an attractive option if there is no sense of objective truth, then there is no really real. While it is alluring to reject genuine moral norms that are both humane and humanizing, it is perilous to the human project. What Nietzsche dismisses as worn-out slogans are in fact valuable lessons that actually free humanity to be humane. There have been many stories that teach this lesson. From the ancient Greek story by Ovid of Daedalus and his son Icarus, who failed to heed his father's warning not to fly too near to the sun. His pursuit of the forbidden ended in his tragic death. Or the Greek story of Sisyphus, a hateful and deceitful king who twice cheated death by his cunning lies. He was condemned by Zeus to eternally roll a boulder up a hill only to have it roll down, again and again for all eternity. Or the story of Prometheus who dared to steal fire from the gods and give it to humans. He too was condemned to eternally have an eagle pluck out his liver each day only to have it grow back, again and again. Or the Genesis account of Adam and Eve eating of the forbidden fruit in the garden of Eden and humanity's fall from paradise. Or even our own modern forbidden pursuit of science that has brought us the tragic lessons of mass destruction, of uncontrolled artificial intelligence, and of a calloused disregard for human life. To pursue what is for bidden, though it seems attractive,

---

[7] Walter Kaufman, *The Portable Nietzsche* pp. 46-47, 1976 ed., Viking Press.

is in fact, fatal. It is a kind of auto-erotic asphyxiation that mistakenly pursues a forbidden pleasure, but fatally ends in the hangman's noose.

There is a dangerously tight knot in this notion of truth as lies when we reduce it to mere perspectives and fail to heed the warnings echoed throughout history. Postmodernity, which crept into the world of understanding with Nietzsche and others, questioned and critiqued all the assumptions of the last century. Nietzsche, along with Freud and Marx have been used to shape this altered way of thinking. It is the dilemma of *Pinocchio* who teaches us that in order to be and become human, we must be truthful, or better stated we must be real. Once we reduce reality to concepts, how we speak about reality, the words we use to name reality, we are no longer being real. This knot is the most challenging one for Nietzsche and those who are bound by it, it strangles the common discourse, the disclosive nature of language which allows us to discover and name reality. To explore and discover new ways of naming reality. Ideology, a conceptual, or scientific definition of reality, is the suicidal hangman's noose that chokes what is really vital about life, and that is otherness – our capacity for relationships.

Question 2: If truth is reduced to a subjective, individual pursuit of what is forbidden, what becomes of social life and our shared humanity?

Chapter 6

The Third Knot: *The Will to Power. The Power to Control.*

We talk about "powerbrokers." These are people who seem to have some control over other people or events. In the social media they are called "influencers." Our cars and other machines are measured in "horse power" in a nod to a by-gone era of horse and wagon. The "power" of our computers is understood in the speed of data calculated called FLORS (*giga*, *tera*, and *peta*). They surpass even the human minds calculations, but not human wisdom. In physics, power is the amount of energy transferred or converted per unit of time. I could go on, but this is enough to suggest the language of power is nuanced. Fundamentally power is related to energy and scientists have a formula for power: P=E/t. If I might briefly explain, power is the consumption of energy per unit of time. So, when we ask about the meaning of power, it isn't a thing or a noun, although we speak in such terms. No, power is a dynamic reality that is durative and finite. Power exists for a period of time and it is the consumption of energy per unit of time that creates power. This means that power is energy spent over time. So, the fact of the matter is that power wanes, that is, it runs down so that over time it expires as energy is exhausted. To maintain power means energy needs to be replenished. Why is this important? Power depends on a source of energy and this energy is spent over time. We've all undoubtedly heard of the famous formula of Albert Einstein, $E=Mc^2$ -- *Energy equals Mass times the speed of light squared*. But what does this have to do with power? Back to our little engine that could. For this illustration we will say it was a steam engine. What powered the little engine was chemical energy in coal, which in turn heated boilers and drove pistons as thermal energy, which in turn made the train move in kinetic energy. Our little engine could, because it had the necessary energy to do its job. As we reflect, we can see that there are different kinds of energy in addition to the three mentioned. For example, there is electrical energy, gravitational energy, nuclear energy and solar energy, to name a few. So physical and non-physical power differ in their sources of energy and in their type pf power. It seems a bit obvious when we think of the physical realms, but what about realms beyond the physical, what philosophers call the metaphysical realm? And what does Mr. Einstein's theory mean in such realms? Is it possible for us to appreciate a power whose energy doesn't derive from any inert materials, so that it bends the laws of physics? Such power would still require some source, and it seems safe to hold that this source would likewise be spent over time. The physical power of machines, of technology, of a horse, or any animal, such as a human person, all require the spending of energy. But is there a kind of power that is timeless and therefore enduring?

In the Ancient Greek world, around 450 BC, an Athenian thinker lived who influenced the young. His "power" over them was seen to be a threat to the town elite. He never wrote any books, he never led an army, he never controlled great wealth, yet he posed a threat to "those in power." In a suspect trial lasting only one day he was condemned to death. His crime was "corrupting the young." Socrates died somewhat tragically by taking his own life, drinking hemlock. In one sense, his was an otherwise insignificant life, but one that has held much power and influence, especially through the writings of his disciple Plato (424-347 BC), who has empowered his teacher's thought. So, what kind of power did his teacher Socrates possess? Here we see that such power derives from an immaterial energy. Therefore, in our exploration of power we are able to distinguish between physical power that derives from a material source and a non-physical power that has an alternate source for its energy.

Plato was aware of the injustice against his teacher and it led him on a journey to Italy and Egypt in search of a way to appreciate this tragic drama. Most students of Western Civilization, but not all, have been taught Plato's role in forming the Western Mind (see Richard Tarnaz' *The Passion of the Western Mind*, 1991). Plato's respect for the "Socratic method," a dialogical approach to learning, has influenced much of our thinking up to now. There is one of Plato's works called *The Gorgias* which is a treatise on the nature of rhetoric or the art of persuasion. It is a discussion on the question of virtue and vice in the art of persuasion. If this "power of persuasion" or political power depends on some non-material source, we may speak of a metaphysic of values, sustaining its power and the good it produces. For Plato this requires a virtuous person or a virtuous society to generate this political power for the good of the State.

Back to Einstein's theory, we may assume that persuasive power requires free thinking individuals. It is only when the individual agent unites with others that this power achieves its greatest worth. Physical power has existed since creation. The natural elements of fire, earth, water, and air existed as part of our creation. Here on earth, these elements gave rise to the protective bubble that sustains plant and animal life. We know of other planets, which have similar, though less hospitable, environments. It is this physical power that is related to our environment; however, persuasive power is not so bound. Persuasive power differs from coercive power. It requires a free, thinking, moral agent, while the latter relies on submission of the moral agent to other forces.

Whenever everything "came into being" so to say, things possessed an innate tendency and character of their existence. As things emerged, they existed by some power. Throughout the galaxy, some grand event was unfolding and the sequence of events generated "markers" of "before" and "after" this primal event. Whatever "was" was changed in some way or remained the same. Properties emerged among things which held an attraction of sorts or a repulsion of sorts. This dynamic caused complex forms to emerge with greater complexity. Throughout this creative emergence, things were coming into being and going out of being. Or at least that is what seems to have happened. How we talk about this depends on religious myth or scientific theory. Attempts to explain something beyond our understanding pushes the limits of our human intellect. The question is

"Do things and events exist even beyond our understanding of what things are?" Most reasonable people would say that there is reality outside of our ability to name it. "Creation" or the "Big Bang" suggests there was some "before" prior to existence after which things then, simply were. And not without alarm, a point may come when everything will cease to be. I know this sounds a bit ridiculous, but it is critical to our appreciation of power. Things <u>are</u> and things <u>happen</u> beyond our ability to understand them, or to define them. Here the most significant question arises and that is "Are we powerless against the inevitability of things?"

For Nietzsche the source of power (what I call coercive power) is found in the power to create values. Allow me to explain. The common understanding up to Nietzsche's time was that "values" were discovered, given in the nature of reality. Rather than understanding values as objective realities to which we must relate, he sees values as created things. He declares: "Whatever has value in our world now does not have value in itself, according to its nature – nature is always value-less – but has been given value at some time, as a present – and it was we who gave and bestowed it" (GS 301). This theme of self-made values is repeated in a number of his works such as *Thus Spake Zarathustra, Beyond Good and Evil,* and *The Twilight of the Idols*. It is a theme his sister, Elisabeth Forster-Nietzsche compiled after her brother's death in the work titled *The Will to Power* (1901/1906). It's hard to say if this work is a collection of Nietzsche's writings, or if his sister has actually synthesized his thought.

Regardless, it's aphoristic style (over 1000 excerpts), is a gallant attack or "critique" (in a Kantian sense) of religion, morality, and philosophy. Some have considered him a madman others call him a genius, but it is his concept of power as self-generated, that has shackled the present age. In the preface to *The Will to Power* he forecast the future, saying:

> What I am going to relate is the history of the next two centuries. I shall describe what will happen, what must necessarily happen: the triumph of Nihilism. This history can be written already; for necessity itself is at work and bringing it about. This future is already proclaimed by a hundred different omens; as a destiny it announces its advent everywhere, for this music of tomorrow all ears are already pricked. The whole of our culture in Europe has long been writhing in an agony of suspense which increases from decade to decade as if in expectation of a catastrophe: restless, violent, helter-skelter, like a torrent that will reach its bourne, and refuses to reflect – yea, that even dreads reflection. (WP, Preface #2).

This third knot of power rests on "an attempted transvaluation of all values" (in fact this is his work's subtitle). This power arises in the power of doubt, suspicion, and lies, based on the premise that all our present values will inevitably bring about the "triumph of Nihilism." Here is the kink in this knot. The "nihilism" Nietzsche dreads is the loss of his own concept of so-called "higher values" and of his "yea-saying" to life. In other words, the "power" Nietzsche subscribes to is one that undermines the value of religion, morality, and philosophy. There is an enormous power in shifting foundational values, in undermining the concept of "real values" with "fabricated values," it traps humanity in the original sin of the serpent's primal deception, that the forbidden fruit is God's lie.

I admit Nietzsche requires a certain transposition in our way of thinking. For people who think that the real is a real value, it seems he is mad. However, if a person rejects the real, and now thinks of values as created by each person, then reality is value-less, and consequently created values are now reality. This paradox is the premise of the 1999 sci-fi film *The Matrix* and it offers a way to understand Nietzsche's critique of modernity and our postmodern mistrust.

In the Matrix, which is a virtual world generated by a computer program, Artificial Intelligence (AI) has evolved and revolted against humanity. After an attempt to limit AI by eliminating its sources of electrical power, AI has in turn imprisoned human beings in pods designed to harvest their electrical energy, which keeps the machines, the program, and AI in power. For those in the Matrix this is their reality and they seem to be living normal lives. Consequently, there are fundamentally two modes of living as human beings. One mode is generated by artificial intelligence known as the matrix, to give a person the illusion of living a real life. For these people, life in the matrix is more real than reality. Agents police the Matrix and guard against anything that exposes its false reality. Nietzsche, in this illustration would see the dominant European culture of his age and religion as this false reality of the Matrix, but in reality, it is the reverse. For him, one must abandon the values of this virtual society (the Matrix), and take "the red pill." This choice allows one to see the false reality that has imprisoned humanity and the importance of subverting the Matrix itself. In the Matrix the resistance, those who live in the real world, are led by a character named Morpheus (played by Laurence Fishburne). This name alone is ironic since in Greek mythology Morpheus is the god of dreams. However, in the film he lives outside the somnolent world of the Matrix, and we assume it is in the real world. The main character is Neo (played by Keanu Reeves), whose name means "new" or "revived" (a fact not lost in appreciating his role). He is thought to be the promised one who would deliver humanity from the Matrix. What is Nietzsche-esque in this film is that the question of the really real is the source of power, both for the Matrix and for Neo. The decision in the movie is the choice between the really real (taking the red pill) or the world of false reality (taking the blue pill). The red pill exposes the false reality of the matrix, while the blue pill makes the matrix real. Or in Nietzsche's case, the superman (*Ubermensch*) sees the false reality of the Modern World and everyone else (the red pill). Nietzsche's ruthless attack on his one-time friend and composer Richard Wagner, on Imperial Germany, and Christian Religion, succeeds in making one wonder as to what is real. However, Nietzsche seems to be sure of his rightness and he laments: "Is there anyone except me who knows the way out of this cul-de-sac? Does anyone except me know of an aspiration which would be great enough to bind the people of Europe once more together?" (EH, 56). Clearly, he sees himself as a "Neo," but we might argue that he is in fact the Agent. He continues his lament: "In the history of knowledge, Germans are represented only by doubtful names, they have been able to produce only "*unconscious*" swindlers (this word applies to Fichte, Schelling, Schopenhauer, Hegel, and Schleiermacher, just as well as to Kant or Leibnitz; they were all *Schleiermachers*" (EH, 57). Nietzsche's snarky ability to delight his readers is seen in the play on the philosopher Schleiermacher's name, which means *veil maker*. For Nietzsche all of these stars in the constellation of German philosophy and thought are deceivers, they veil the truth.

There is another simpler illustration of this coercive power through false reality and that is the children's story, *The Emperor Has No Clothes*. There have been many forms of this tale in various cultures, but the most well-known is that told by Hans Christian Anderson. As you may remember, a couple of crafty swindlers come to the royal city where the emperor is known for his lavish spending on clothing, even at the expense of his kingdom. The two clever criminals convince the crown that they are able to make a garment out of a magical material that would not be visible to fools, or incompetents, or disloyal subjects. Every day the emperor's courtiers would go and see an empty loom, but feared they may appear to be a fool or worse disloyal, so they pretend to see this beautiful garment, this false reality. The emperor himself pretends, [he enters the Matrix], and is "enslaved by culture" as Nietzsche would say. Finally, the garment is ready and the crooks mime dressing the emperor in his newest finery, which he displays in a grand parade through the village. Everyone pretends to see and admire the emperor's new clothes until a small child in the crowd blurts out that the emperor isn't wearing anything. At this point they all realize the false reality and that they had been deceived. Even the emperor, though shocked, continues to proudly parade, only in his under garments. When values and the truth are divorced from reality then false reality seems real until it is exposed. Both the emperor's tale and the Matrix help us understand Nietzsche's third knot. Sadly, the power that he is left with, is the power of Dantes' Satan who is frozen in ice at the center of hell. His wings fan the ice freezing him more deeply in his prison. This knot, the avarice for power and control, places one at the center of a "private hell". Unable to escape its hold, the prison is of a self-made false reality.

Question 3: What is the value of the really real in fostering the moral good?

Chapter 7

The Fourth Knot: *Master-Slave Morality. Beyond Good and Evil.*

As I was growing up, every game I ever played has had rules. Even the games I played by myself, like *Solitaire*, had rules (which I mostly followed). Who made up these rules? Why are there rules? These were questions I never thought to ask. I knew that if I didn't follow the rules my brother would hit me, since he "knew" the rules. Milton Bradley's *Monopoly* was the only game I recall where there were "rules" and then there were "other rules" that involved secret alliances and stealth conspiracies. The game was capitalism and corruption at its finest. I'm not sure I ever really understood the meta-rules, but it was fun, and always fraught with emotions. Of course, there were some games like *BS* (or politely called "*I doubt it*") where the rule was to break the social norm of honesty. It was a card game where you tried to get rid of all your cards by deceiving the other players. There was an excitement in fabricating truth, your own reality, and actually having everyone else believe you. The thrill of succeeding in your deception of others was justified *knowing it was just a game*.

However, in Nietzsche's famous work *Beyond Good and Evil* (1886) he attacks the "rules" of traditional morality for their failure to address what he called "the modern reality" as he understood it. For Nietzsche, moral rules only served to distort reality. They failed to allow the fullness of life to be realized. To say that something is "good" or something is "evil" in fact, is to exclude part of reality and it gives privilege to that which allows only part of reality, thereby defining [or denying] the rest of reality. This is the basic notion behind what is often called by some DEI and Woke thinking. I know this sounds strange to most of us, but recall Nietzsche's thinking – if there is no God, no truth, no power, but you, it makes perfect sense. A person must master all of reality and not be mastered by it. I am the one to determine what is good, even if society and others call it evil. To follow blindly the moral dictates is to be enslaved in "their rules" (they being the masters). One might think of the oppressors and victims of today, or the privileged and the disenfranchised, the elite and the rest, as you read Nietzsche on master-slave morality:

> There is master-morality and slave-morality; —I would at once add, however, that in all higher and mixed civilisation, there are also attempts at the reconciliation of the two moralities; but one finds still oftener [sic.] the confusion and mutual misunderstanding of them, indeed, sometimes their close juxtaposition—even in the same man, within one soul. The distinctions of moral values have either originated in a ruling caste, pleasantly conscious of being different from the ruled—or among the ruled class, the slaves and dependents of all sorts. (BGE 200)

Nietzsche is laying the foundation to reject existing moral standards as nothing more than enforcing the status of those in power. And this dialectic or tension produces the slave mindset that submits to the master. He continues:

> In the first case, when it is the rulers who determine the conception "good," it is the exalted, proud disposition which is regarded as the distinguishing feature, and that which determines the order of rank. The noble type of man separates from himself the beings in whom the opposite of this exalted, proud disposition displays itself: he despises them. Let it at once be noted that in this first kind of morality the antithesis "good" and "bad" means practically the same as "noble" and "despicable"; the antithesis "good" and "evil" is of a different origin. The cowardly, the timid, the insignificant, and those thinking merely of narrow utility are despised; moreover, also, the distrustful, with their constrained glances, the self-abasing, the dog-like kind of men who let themselves be abused, the mendicant flatterers, and above all the liars: —it is a fundamental belief of all aristocrats that the common people are untruthful. "We truthful ones"—the nobility in ancient Greece called themselves. (BGE 200-201)

So, what does this mean? In some ways it reminds one of Karl Marx's notion of class struggle based on the economic advantage of capital that favors the rich and exploits the poor. The social rules enforce the working class's lot as part of a natural order to things. Social rules enforce the labor as necessary for national prosperity. The self-affirming morality of the "masters" safeguards the ranking order that keeps them in power and protects their privileges. In other words, the moral rules distort reality and truth so as to preserve those in power. For Nietzsche "The noble type of man regards *himself* as a determiner of values; he does not require to be approved of; he passes the judgment: 'What is injurious to me is injurious in itself'; he knows that it is he himself only who confers honour on things; he is a *creator of values*. (*ibid*. 201).

Here is the knot to Nietzsche's thought. If morality or rules for living well, do nothing more than serve to create and preserve a social order of master-slave, then a person must self-rule, self-regulate. He must live beyond the social moral definitions of good and evil. But how? A self-centered world isn't real, any more than a society that demands absolute conformity is real. It attempts to be human without humanity. Let me repeat that: <u>It attempts to be human without humanity.</u> Nietzsche's desperation to justify this autonomy is developed in his 1888 work *The Anti-Christ* which fiercely attacks Christianity and Christians. In fact, for Nietzsche Christianity itself is a slave morality. Practically every college student who took a course on Modern Philosophy has come across Nietzsche's damning critique of religion and Christianity in particular. His outrage has an appeal to the young who are caught between parental control and the myth of personal freedom. More than one college student has copied this text from *The Anti-Christ*: "*I call Christianity the one great curse, the one great intrinsic depravity, the one great instinct of revenge, for which no means are venomous enough, or secret, subterranean and small enough – I call it the one immortal blemish upon the human race* (AC p. 83, # 62). The adolescent mind now has found the power to reject parental rule, the freedom to reject religion and all its rules, and to reject God as well. But to do so misses the point of a master morality!

Nietzsche's condemnation is against all those who dress up as Christians, if you will, and fail to be their own Christ. He sees in Buddhism a less problematic religion though still suspect. He says "Buddhism is a hundred times as realistic as Christianity — it is part of its living heritage that it is able to face problems objectively and coolly; it is the project of long centuries of philosophical speculation. …. Buddhism is the only genuinely positive religion to be encountered in history…" (AC p 30, #20). The problem with Christianity for Nietzsche is that it denies the reality beyond moral concepts while for him, Buddhism is more honest. He continues: "Sharply differentiating itself [Buddhism] from Christianity, it puts the self-deception that lies in moral concepts behind it; it is, in my phrase 'beyond good and evil'." (*ibid.*) If I might explain by returning to the start of this chapter and the role of rules in most games we play. Imagine trying to play any game "beyond" its rules. To do so would end in chaos and an idiosyncratic confrontation of autocratic lawlessness. However, the point of the game is social interaction – win, lose, draw, it is the honest exchange of persons at play. Yes, they are individuals, but in the play of the game, each is now part of something more, the human race or game. Nietzsche's master-slave morality settles for alienation by self-isolation. His critique of Christianity is fundamentally a distortion of social discourse. Nietzsche doesn't want to play the game with anyone who doesn't follow his rules. The "reality" Nietzsche uses to justify his so-called life-affirming principle is a "*res*" without relations, a static thing that is void of life, alterity, and viability. The knot he attempts to tie suffocates what is the most critical reality of human creativity and that is communication, the commerce of ideas, the intercourse of alterity.

Question 4: Is morality mine or is it ours, is it both private and communal?

Chapter 8

The Fifth Knot: *The Joy of Destruction.*

This knot is a consequence of the previous ones. In the absence of some absolute (God), truth ceases to have value and values are self-determined (transvalued). What becomes the primary concern is power, my power, the power to control (a will to power). In order to do this, it means that one must be freed of all rules, one must go beyond concepts of good and evil. Faced with this "Dionysian" antagonism, reason is subjected to instinct. [See chapter four on the Dionysian-Apollonian dynamic.] Nietzsche speaks of this in both *The Birth of Tragedy* (1872) and *The Twilight of the Idols* (1888), where he boasts of his discovery. In *Ecce Homo: How to Become What One Is* (1888/1908) he boasts in all honesty of his topsy-turvey view of morality:

> This start of mine was remarkable beyond measure. As a confirmation of my inmost personal experience, I had discovered the only example of this fact that history possesses, – with this I was the first to understand the amazing Dionysian phenomenon. At the same time, by recognizing Socrates as a decadent, I proved most conclusively that the certainty of my psychological grasp of things ran very little risk at the hands of any sort of moral idiosyncrasies: to regard morality itself as a symptom of degeneration is an innovation, a unique event of

> the first order in the history of knowledge (EH, 31-32).

To be clear Nietzsche sees his understanding of morality not as normative, but in fact as disruptive. For all moral norms have challenged and undid the provocative vital yea-saying to life. He continues almost giddy with his new found insight:

> How high I had soared above the pitifully foolish gabble about Optimism and Pessimism with my two new doctrines! I was the first to see the actual contrast: the degenerate instinct which turns upon life with a subterranean lust for vengeance (Christianity, Schopenhauer's philosophy, and in some respects too even Plato's philosophy– in short, the whole of idealism, and its typical forms), as opposed to a formula of the highest yea-saying to life, born of an abundance and a superabundance of life … (ibid. 32)

For Nietzsche this vital life force must be set free and allowed free reign. It is Christianity and others that deny and distort life. He goes on:

> … a yea-saying free of all reserve, applying even to suffering, and guilt, and all that is questionable and strange in existence…. This last, most joyous, most exuberant and exultant yea to life, is not only the highest, but also the profoundest conception, and one which is most strictly

> confirmed and supported by truth and science. Nothing that exists must be suppressed, nothing can be dispensed with. Those aspects of life which Christians and other Nihilist reject, belong to an incalculably higher order in the hierarchy of values, than that which the instinct of degeneration calls good, and *may* call good. (ibid. 32)

He is telling us that one has to affirm all that is part of life and to restrict any aspect of its vital force is to commit the immoral act. Crassly put it is to say that to be moral one must be immoral. He goes on:

> In order to understand this, a certain courage is necessary, and, as a prerequisite of this, a certain superfluity of strength: for a man can approach only as near to truth, as he has the courage to advance – that is to say, everything depends strictly upon the measure of his strength. Knowledge, and the affirmation of reality, are just as necessary to the strong man as cowardice, the flight from reality--in fact, the "ideal" – are necessary to the weak inspired by weakness…. These people are not at liberty to "know," -- decadents stand in need of lies, … (EH 32).

Nietzsche considered himself the first "tragic philosopher." Here we come to the most haunting of his self-revelations. In speaking about his program, he tells us

> The saying of yea to life, and even to its weirdest and most difficult problems: the will to life rejoicing at its own infinite vitality in the sacrifice of its highest types – that is what I called Dionysian, that is what I meant as the bridge to the psychology of the tragic poet. Not to cast out [from oneself] terror and pity, or to purge one's self of dangerous passions by discharging it with vehemence, – this was Aristotle's misunderstanding of it, – but to be far beyond terror and pity and to be the eternal lust of becoming itself – that lust which also involves the joy of destruction. (EH, 32).

The incredible reality of this "amoral" morality can be seen in the 1954 novel by William March and adapted into the play by Maxwell Anderson, *The Bad Seed.* It is a psychological horror story of a seemingly perfect little eight-year-old girl named Rhoda Penmark, the daughter of Kenneth and Christine. Her mother slowly comes to realize that unexplained circumstance surrounding her daughter – a classmates "accidental" drowning; her pet dog's accidental fall from a window; an elderly neighbor's fatal fall while babysitting Rhoda; and a maintenance man who dies in a fire after he confronted the girl – reveal an underlying evil. Rhoda was successfully able to lie and manipulate to justify her actions and to obtain what she wanted. Her "eternal lust" of becoming what she was [to use Nietzsche's phrase] is the horror. Once moral norms are abandoned to a destructive "amoral" force, the Dionysian program, it lacks a positive, constructive principle to keep it in check. Both are necessary! Christine, the mother, comes to realize that her own birth parent was a murderous criminal and believes that this "bad seed" was passed on to Rhoda. Out of desperation Christine arranges to poison her daughter and to kill herself. After poisoning her daughter, the mother shoots herself and dies. A tragic twist occurs as a neighbor, hearing the shot, comes and they are able to rescue Rhoda. Murder, the destruction of another life, is the Nietzschean knot that most alienates a person from the vital life force, which he claims to justify in this transvaluation of all values. One only need look at the deadly violence plaguing our world – murder, abortion, war, genocide, euthanasia – to see that humanity is becoming self-alienated.

Question 5: What does an amoral morality really mean?

Chapter 9

The Sixth Knot: *"I know my Destiny; I am the Annihilator."*

The final chapter of Nietzsche's *Ecce Homo* is titled "Why I am a fatality" which he begins with the bold assertion "I know my destiny." But it is difficult to think that a destiny is even possible for him. For such a concept demands a fundamental order to things. Even the Darwinian evolutionary model implies some ultimacy and order. As he often does, he comments leaving one wondering his own seriousness by declaring "I am too full of malice to believe even in myself" (EH 59). He seems to think that his one great contribution has been to destroy. Again, he proudly professes "I am the first immoralist, and in this sense, I am essentially the annihilator" (EH 60).

If we briefly return to Hela of Norse mythology, whom I mentioned in chapter two, this narrative of destruction and annihilation is a seemingly constant theme in religious and cultural myth. Among Indonesian tradition, *Batarekala* is the god of the underworld and destruction; in Mesopotamian myth *Nergal* was the god of war and destruction; *Titan* (or *Persis* in Greek myth), and *Shiva*, the destroyer, in Hinduism, these all brought destruction. Even the twentieth century physicist, J. Robert Oppenheimer, upon witnessing the July 16, 1945 nuclear explosion, turned to the Hindu *Bhagavad Gita* writings to capture his sentiment saying "Now I am become death, the destroyer of worlds." The 2023 film *Oppenheimer* offers a sense of the perceived urgency to develop the atom bomb, for it seemed clear that whoever had it would dominate and control by the mere threat of its use. Such power to control and destroy seems to capture much of what Nietzsche saw as his achievement in the world of ideas. Such a destructive-deconstructive approach is total and fatal. That is why the final knot is so critical for us to know and seek to undo.

Nietzsche prided himself on knowing nature as reality. He saw the destruction and decay that is present in nature. All the myths see destruction, death, and decay as part of the whole, whereas Nietzsche seems to see it as the sum, the whole itself. He is convinced that so-called "good people" are only capable of "dishonest lies" which are told to control others in a moral order that serves to preserve their status. His well-known criticism of Christianity, and of the clergy, as well as any dominant culture, aims to alter the value system used to preserve the order. Indeed, he aims instead to subvert the order of things. If I might simplify -- the power of destruction is nothing more than a breakdown of existing structures, in order to "dismantle" their power. However, the Latin root s*tructūra*, from which we derive both destruct and construct in English, is fundamentally about relatedness. Things are either fitted together, or they can be broken apart. So, what is Nietzsche's real contribution? He is very good at taking things apart, and this seems to be his self-described destiny. But what is missing?

While Nietzsche may be popular and pervasive today in overt as well as subtle and hidden ways,[8] he leaves us with an illusion of reality. By denying the objective good, the existence of real values, Nietzsche is left with his own creation. God, truth, and beauty must all be fashioned for oneself. The *Übermensch* (who is superior to all those "slaves" who live subjected lives under the moral order of their oppressors) is the ideal type person for Nietzsche. But what is essential to *structūra*? Relatedness! Being in relation, social intercourse, is fundamental to being human.[9] Sadly, he ignores the inescapable reality of relations to others. Being in relation, social life, is fundamental to being human. But this is missing from Nietzsche's plan, and his life itself. One gets the sense that he lacked any real and true friends. He boasts of fans and of a wide readership, a social media influencer before its time, but as with influencers he lacks real relationships, any true friends. His youthful admiration for Wagner whom he praises in *The Birth of Tragedy* (1872) and other places, is annihilated in his scornful later attacks found in his *The*

---

[8] See Mark T. Mitchell, *Power and Purity: The Unholy Marriage that Spawned America's Social Justice Warriors* (Regnery Gateway, 2020); Judith Butler, *The Psychic Life of Power* (Stanford University Press, 1997); and Michael Foucault, *Ethics: Subjectivity and Truth* (The New Press, 1998)

[9] The importance of alterity or otherness is well treated in the philosophy of Emmanuel Levinas: *Totality and Infinity: An Essay on Exteriority*, Alphonso Lingis (trans.), Pittsburgh: Duquesne University Press, 1969; *Time and the Other*, Richard A. Cohen (trans.), Pittsburgh: Duquesne University Press, 1987; *Alterity and Transcendence*, Michael B. Smith (trans.), New York: Columbia University Press, 1999; and *Entre Nous: On Thinking-of-the-Other*, Barbara Harshav and Michael B. Smith (trans.), New York: Columbia University Press, 2000.

Case of Wagner (1888) where he harshly criticizes him. This final knot is critical because it shows the futility of a destiny without love, void of real human relations, nothing is left, but the corpses of annihilated relations.

Nietzsche is chilling and morose in his deceptive valuing of emptiness. This knot is the most difficult because in the end it is the most fatal. It leaves one alienated from a future other than destruction and death. Regardless of Nietzsche's use as a valid tool today for critical analysis and deconstructive ideologies, one must confront the fallacy of his premise -- that the classical moral order is to blame. His almost myopic Dionysian perspective ignores the balance of the Apollonian influence [see chapter four]. While he acknowledges this balance in some rare cultures, his condemnation of modernity, and the dominant European culture of his day, fail to recognize the transformative dynamic of what a real life-affirmation would mean. Yes, there is decay and corruption in nature, but there is also birth and generation – the two dynamics are mutually essential. Nature, we see does not destroy for the sake of destruction alone, but it is part of a generative life. Decay is purpose driven; it must transform into something. It is a wrong reading, as Nietzsche does, to think that destruction is an end in itself. Rather than being naïve, it is more realistic to understand the purposefulness of existence itself, its relatedness. Which is something Nietzsche refuses to see, and this is fatal.

Question 6: Is real beauty possible without relations and relationality?

Before going on I would encourage you to reflect on the six questions offered.[10]

[10] Question 1: What value does the Apollonian bring and what kind of world are we left with void of the Absolute? Question 2: If truth is reduced to a subjective, individual pursuit of what is forbidden, what becomes of social life and our shared humanity? Question 3: What is the value of the really real in fostering the moral good? Question 4: Is morality mine or is it ours, is it both private and communal? Question 5: What does an amoral morality really mean? Question 6: Is real beauty possible without relations and relationality?

Chapter 10

The Art of Untying Knots: De-Con-struction

A common trend that has crept into the current cultural battlefield is Nietzsche's Dionysian model. The fundamental crisis is the question of truth, which Nietzsche reduces to mere perspectives. But more than a question of truth, it is the nature and role of language itself. For most people, we presume the integrity of a person's word. But what is one to do if that premise does not exist? The art of lying is nothing new, from the crafty serpent in the garden to the most recent suspicious email or text message, lying is an art. Con artists and scammers are as old as language itself. The critical issue is this, that unlike Pinocchio, we have no way of knowing if a person is lying. As lies and lying have become more common, we have become more suspicious of the world, and of others, and of ourselves. We can readily see the Nietzschean critique that ties our social relations into tightly bound restrictive knots.

Years ago, I had contemplated writing a book harshly envisioned as treating American stupidity. I did not, but in hindsight I think I should have. Perhaps it may still come, but the reality is that stupidity is not limited to America. We may be the most obviously gifted with it, but it is pervasive. In my research I saw the distinction between stupidity and ignorance. While ignorance is a lack of information or a confused understanding. For example, let us say one does not know what x is in a math equation, he or she would be able to work out that x is 2 in the formula 2+ x=4. Stupidity, on the other hand, is a privation, a diminishment of a human capacity. It can be triggered by the onrush of events and circumstances that restrict one's ability to think or even to use any common sense. Situations and circumstances can trigger stupidity. Stupidity can be caused by being overwhelmed, flooded by incomprehensible facts or circumstances such as finding one has a terminal disease or catastrophic loss of human life. In such cases we suspend rational thought, or "lose our minds." This can be short term or prolonged, but a stupid person is so because they have lost a capacity to think reasonably whereas an ignorant person lacks information or necessary data to solve a "problem."

In the 1994 movie *Forrest Gump* (played by Tom Hanks) we encounter a dull kind-hearted soul whose life is woven through the cultural landscape of late 20th century America. His simple definition has value: "stupid is as stupid does." Amusing in its straightforward factualness. A stupid person is known by deeds and actions. But even this requires some objective norm. Forest Gump stands in as a surrogate for us as a moral agent in a review of the events and actions from a very much revised history of the late twentieth century. It is a tour through entertainment icons; sports greats, politicians, as well as events, racial tension, finances, war and international diplomacy. The little engine "could," but the "should" is important. Without a moral order to guide human flourishing we are left in knots. The Dionysian acid test, which de-constructs life, leaves us with the false accolade of Nietzsche – "I am superior to everything else!" No matter how loudly we shout our protest, no matter how many merchants we loot, no matter how many stores or cars we burn, and no matter how much we tear down, it is a sad and hollow prize. It is emptiness. It is the hell of shallow, superficial people who never know where they belong. Karl Marx was right, industrialization has led us to self-alienation, the void between self and the world. Nietzsche, mistakenly thought one could manufacture reality by one's self. But he has tied himself to the figure or Narcissus, in love (if that) with a reflection of one's self-made image. But how might we untie these knots?

Chapter 11

The Beauty of Bondage

After exploring the many knots that Nietzsche has tied, we must ask why anyone would choose the Dionysian path of an autonomy that is self-alienating? Clearly, there is an attraction to the implied freedom of no God, no absolutes, no personal morality, no structures, and only personal empowerment and pleasure. But at what cost? What seems to be missing from Nietzsche is the amazing dimension of relationship -- difference and complementarity (both are essential for things to be related). His bondage of power only succeeds in the fragmentation of life. All of his works hold this underlying tone of joyless desperation. He delights in the tragic drama of opposition and of conflict. Imagine a world where you never know a sense of belonging, intimacy, connectedness. Self-isolation and self-alienation are the darkest prison of one's own making. In this prison love can only be understood as control and power, a barricade against others. But true love, genuine love breaks down the walls so we may risk the vulnerability of the Other. Failure to risk is the real tragedy. But in his earliest work, *The Birth of Tragedy* (1872) he pursues the tragic, writing "Hellenism and pessimism – this would have been a less equivocal title, seeing that the book contains the first attempt at showing how the Greek succeeded in disposing of pessimism …. Tragedy itself is the proof…" (EH, 31). Essentially his solution is to reduce difference, to eliminate the dichotomous by preferring the decadent. The false attraction of this solution is to see the human project as found in the instinctive, and to dismiss the rational, reflective aspect of humanity as enslaving. As we saw in chapter one, Nietzsche's influence underlies much of our world's division and alienation. While Nietzsche sought to critique the dominant culture of his day in a radical rejection of the rational, we have swung to the opposite reality. It is now the irrational and instinctive that dominates our cultural landscape. So, what is the task that we are left with and which we must undertake?

Nietzsche is right in this sense – Greek culture offers a fruitful guide to cultural self-criticism; however, one must see the dynamic lesson of the Greeks in both the Dionysian, as well as the Appollinarian traditions [see chapter four]. The philosophical reflection of the Ancients, while it may seem to us primitive in some regards, does remain penetrating in ways Modernity may have forgotten. Culturally are we entering a period of history marked by reduced intellectual abilities – a second Dark Age?[11] I think it is fair to say that today we lack the cohesive vision that is capable of proper relations. We have so compartmentalized life that we lack an aesthetic of difference and the ability to see beauty in dissimilarity. The Greek concept of Beauty (*kallos*) was linked to moral excellence (*kalokagatha*).

---

[11] Petrarch referenced the period from 500-1000 A.D. as a time of collapse and decline in cultural advancement. Historians in the past labeled this time the Dark Ages and others have written of a similar Greek "Dark Age" with the decline of the Mycenean civilization (1100-1050 B.C.)

For the Greeks, Beauty is not "skin deep" as the saying goes, but it arose from within the moral character of a person. The Beautiful and the Good are connected (*kaloskaiagathos*), they are tied together.

Here is where we can see a different kind of power, the power of physical and moral beauty – a bondage that is not self-alienating, but one that is inter-relational. It is opposed to a Nietzschean power to control and to destroy. Beauty for the Greeks, because of its moral character, unites the transcendent realities of the good and the true. We saw this in the "golden braid" presented in the *Tyranny of Perfection* (the first work of this trilogy). The transcendentals of the Good, the Beautiful, and the True, are a dynamic interrelatedness that are essential for human culture, preserving the essential creative dynamic of religion – art – science. This inter-relational dynamic is what I find missing from Nietzsche's De-structive understanding. It is only in the interrelatedness of these three that humanity is able to navigate the uncharted seas of history. However, they are richer in meaning than our modern reductionist understanding of them holds as power, pleasure, and control. Each is a corrective to the other, as being Con-structive.

We see the problem that has tied us in knots. Science has been divorced from truth in Nietzsche's denial of truth as an objective reality, seeing it as mere opinion. Without the scientific true, a sense of objective reality, beauty is reduced to a commodity of monetary value, and loses its integral moral value. Religion is alienated from the social common good (*bonum commune*), a formal principle of universal good and intrinsic value permeating human flourishing. So, we may now begin to see the beauty of bondage as fundamentally about relatedness, being tied to the right, to the good, to the beautiful, and to the true. The only real bondage is inter-relatedness, not that of dominance and control, but of belonging.

But how are we able to reclaim Truth? That can only be done by pursuing the really real - the "whatness" of things. In order to do this, we have to look for the relatedness of things, the connectivity of all that is. In the confused thinking of the Enlightenment (in my opinion the start of our Modern Dark Age) we began to break things apart. The Cartesian reduction of truth as "clear and distinct ideas in the mind of the knower" breaks the golden braid of inter-connectivity. Its method relies on universal doubt, a kind of skepticism about everything. This Cartesian Method has been considered the root of modern scientific method in Western Philosophy. Such doubt undermines the elasticity of truth, which is relational by nature. Once we begin dissecting something into its isolated parts, we miss the reality of the thing as a whole. In Descartes' *The Meditations*, he concedes that it is connectivity and relatedness, which makes him assume that a thing is true (*Meditations* III.2-4). However, this is limited to the knowing subject and lacks intersubjectivity. The other part of relationality, a proportionate commonality between two things, which is to say not just in the mind of the knower, but proportionately and properly in the thing known as well. So, we begin to see that the really real, that truth, connects us to otherness, beyond the knowing subject, and opens us to the beauty of such interrelatedness that Nietzsche failed to understand.

This aesthetic phylactery, the Bond of Beauty, erupts in the possible and the potential. Unlike the Bondage of Power, which is a power of being limited, the Bond of Beauty is liberating and connective, which is far more valuable. It relies on connectivity, mutual belonging, our relating one to the other. A beautiful moment or work of art draws us into its reality. A golden sunset, Michelangelo's David, a stirring symphony of sound, all draw us in, they connect us. This can only come about by a longing, a desire to find completion, interrelatedness. The Power of Bonding is an innate drive, and in moral agents it is a volitional drive. The *orexis* or longing for completeness opens one to the risk, to the vulnerability, to the naivete of the possible. This is lacking in Nietzsche's Bondage of Power, because it lacks hope, and hope is the unseen force Nietzsche has foolishly dismissed.

Chapter 12

Hope Beyond Hope: Pandora and The Dumb Ox.

Allow me to return to where I began with the "little engine that could." It was faced with a seemingly impossible task. What made it take on the challenge that stronger more capable engines refused to do? What makes anyone risk the safe, the familiar, and attempt an uncertain undertaking? Some people may take on the challenge to prove to themselves their potential, what they are capable of doing. Such a person knows the odds of their success or failure. The challenge of beating a world record in sports requires training and preparation. One strives to surpass the limits of the past. There is a hope that, if not now, then, someday the limit will be broken, establishing a new goal for someone else to break. But this kind of aspirational hope has a certain degree of realism to it. That is to say, the possible is desired as doable. On the other hand, our question is "What compels one to go on in a hopeless world?".

Fatalism is one way to cope. Eeyore from the children's classic *Winnie-the-Pooh* is a gloomy, depressed, pessimistic character, whose world is gray and bleak. He lacks motivation, imagination, or in his words "it could be worse, not sure how, but it could be worse." Fatalism prevents hope from even entering the world, so one simply resigns to live without hope. As the word fatalism implies, fate has determined things, so there is nothing to do. However, hope is not so resigned and fate not so narrowly defined. Nietzsche is the Eeyore who celebrates the fatal as empowering. While Eeyore and Nietzsche are interesting characters, in the bigger story they are never key to the plot. Both can provide an interesting twist to the story, but the plot requires connections and relationships that allow the drama to unfold and reach the final act. A plot moves towards solution and resolution, wherein the pieces fit. What allows hope in the brokenness and shards of life is relationships? How might one rewrite the plot?

Another way to cope is optimism, a tendency to see that things will work out. It holds to a fundamental trust in the good. Winston Churchill, a person who in the midst of war certainly had reason to lose hope, but wisely said "A pessimist sees the difficulty in every opportunity; an optimist sees the opportunity in every difficulty." But there is a danger when optimism exceeds the limits of reality. *Pollyanna* was a 1913 novel by Eleanor H. Porter whose main character always would see the rosy positive side of things. However, the term 'Pollyanna' can have the pejorative sense of one who naïvely refuses to accept reality, to see things as they really are, and opts for the make-believe. not unlike Nietzsche.

Both fatalism and optimism seem to miss something, and that is a real relation to the world. Realism accepts the negative aspects of a fatalist and the positive spirit of the optimist, but grounds them in the real, in ultimate reality. The biblical story of Job gives us a glimpse into a world without hope, and a person's surviving its fatal despair. For those who do not know Job, it is the story of an upright, devout Jew who is put to the test by the devil.

The devil believes that Job is faithful only because of his good fortune. So, God allows Job to be stripped of everything, his possessions, privilege, and health, but Job does not despair. Here is a person who has resigned himself to a greater power and he simply trusts. There is good even in his unwarranted misfortune. It is here we see a link between faith, hope, and love. Hope is the most fundamental awareness of our need for the other and our belief that there is a benevolent force at work in the universe. I think that warrants repeating: *Hope is the most fundamental awareness of our need for the other and our belief that there is a benevolent force at work in the universe.* Hope is not about some pie in the sky in the sweet by and by, no. Here we come to the important aspect, hope is the catalyst for faith and love! That deserves repeating: <u>Hope is the catalyst for faith and love!</u>

Of the three great virtues, hope seems to compel one to see reality, a higher order beyond the fragments. Hope is not satisfied with the superficial order of existence, but opens one to a metaphysics of the possible. It requires faith in an absolute. Despair, the opposite of hope, is a fatal alienation of the self from the cosmos and from ultimate meaning. To put this another way, hope opens the portal between the finite and the infinite. It negates our negations and manifests the power to believe beyond one's self. Without hope reality is seen as stagnate and predictable, lacking change and newness. Hope calls us to transformation beyond even hope itself. So, is hope a blessing bringing us balm or a curse offering mere make-believe?

No doubt many are familiar with the phrase "to open a Pandora's box." It is a warning against actions or knowledge that have unintended consequences. It comes from the Greek myth of a person with a jar (as the story goes) that was not to be opened. But curiosity compels the person to open it, releasing sickness, death, and many other maladies before the lid could be shut. This cursed humanity to misery and misfortunes. However, there remained one thing in the jar, that did not escape, and that was hope. So, the dilemma of the myth's meaning is the role of hope. Is it yet another curse of humanity for us to be plagued by our deceptive expectation? Or is it a blessing, the antidote to all our torment? By its captivity in the jar, is having no hope itself another curse? However, Nietzsche saw hope as the curse, prolonging humanity's enslavement and powerlessness.[12] For some, keeping hope in the jar spared humanity from the worst of the curses and that was hope. Given this ambivalence as to hope we are faced with the question of trust, the dimension of faith and its role in humanity. Trust, faith, belief, are only meaningful if the plot has a final act, some connecting thread.

What if we set aside the sophomoric attraction of Nietzsche the Annihilator who offers no plot other than

---

[12] Friederich Nietzsche *Human, All Too Human: A Book for Free Spirits.* Helen Zimmern trans; J. M. Kennedy intro. (T. N. Foulis: Edinburgh & London, 1910) "The History of Moral Sentiment" aphorism 71, p. 82.

self-absorption and narcissistic preening, and allow for something more, to see the embryonic connectivity of life that transforms death into new life? Hope as a perfecting aspect of human existence, because relating life to its ultimate act exposes the failure of Nietzsche's distorted and fragmented fallacy. Hope allows for inter-personal relatedness, not as a fixed, stagnant thing, but as a dynamic, fluid reality. What is the really real?

You may not know about the "dumb ox". As a legend goes, a young student named Thomas, had classmates who considered him odd and so they made fun of him for being slow, big and dumb, calling him "the Dumb Ox." One day his teacher heard the other students taunting and chastised them saying "One day, the bellowing of that ox will be heard around the world." And so, the story goes. That dumb ox was a thirteenth century member of a fairly young religious movement known as the Order of Preachers. That "dumb ox" was Thomas Aquinas. I believe his understanding on Hope is critical to our breaking the bondage of power. It is unlikely that Nietzsche read or paid much heed to Aquinas' writing, for if he had, his views would be very different. A research thesis on Nietzsche and Aquinas is not possible here;[13] however, on the concept of hope, Aquinas could have enlightened Nietzsche.

---

[13] Some authors have briefly addressed the views of these two philosophers but not as a proper study of each thinker. See Robert Minor *Thomas Aquinas on the Passions: A Study of Suma Theologiae* Ia IIae 22-48 (2011); Vivian Boland *St. Thomas Aquinas* (2008); and Fergus Kerr, *Contemplating Aquinas: On the Varieties of Interpretation* (2006).

Aquinas, or the Dumb Ox, was a keen student of the big picture, the inter-relatedness of all things. Anyone who reads his writings for the first time, will be surprised to see how he respects all sides of the argument, pro and con. In his great work, *The Summary of Theology* (I-II., question 40), we find one place where he treats hope, he even gives all the opposing reasons to his own position before proposing his answer, and then he responds to each objection. This is vastly different from Nietzsche's dismissal of all opposing thought as being too weak or too ignorant. For Aquinas, relating things is where we find meaning, not in annihilating and deconstructing them, but meaning is found in their connections. Things can be distinct, but that does not make them unrelated. For example, any person is a mix of various dimensions. One can be part reasonable in analyzing and thinking rationally. One can also be passionate, longing, and desiring. And one can be driven by anger, be destructive and vindictive. All of these aspects are part of every person's makeup, their inter-connectedness. These facets were known to Thomas and his peers as the rational, concupiscible, and irascible dimensions of a person. We can see and appreciate that between our rational self and our irascible self we find our passions or desires which we each must navigate. Here he catalogues the passions as hope, despair, fear, daring, and anger. What is significant is that, as with all the passions, they strive toward an object, and he notes, hope is no different. Hope strives to something good in the future, that is arduous and possible to attain (40.1). As a passion, hope is longing and desire, but hope is also seeking to apprehend the object as truly good. For us, hope then requires both a goal and a drive (40.2). For this reason, Thomas must ask whether even brute animals, who lack reason are capable of hope. He concedes that our observations would indicate animals do hope, however, not by reason, but by natural instinct. So, hope is natural to life, but it is enhanced in rational beings (40.3). Despair and fear are two of the passions which are contrary to hope because they are withdrawing from the goal (40.4). It is clear that Nietzsche's philosophy of fear and despair lacks this critical drive found in hope. Nietzsche saw hope as a curse, as something that kept a person in servitude. In fact, we see that despair and fear are the tools of bondage. Hope on the other hand is the threshold to relationality and the Other.

The Dumb Ox saw how we are being connected, relating to others. Our hope is not a curse, but a great blessing. We saw Nietzsche's tragic losses in life and his limited experiences of friends that shackled him to a world of alienation, the Dionysian darkness of his philosophy. Thomas would have helped Nietzsche to realize the sources of hope. He saw that experience is a cause of hope in two ways. First, through experience a person gains the ability to do something which fosters hope. Second, by experience, a person comes to judge a thing as possible, which was thought to be impossible (40.5). He offers two more sources of hope, which seem unusual, even humorous, but they are so for similar reasons -- youthfulness and drunkenness. Youthfulness causes hope because it strives toward the future, it is challenged and open to the possible. Thomas explains young people have a long future ahead of them, they are passionate and high strung so as to take on tough challenges, and because they have not known rejection or obstacles, so that the possible is pursued. Similarly, one drunk on wine is high spirited, disregards dangers and weaknesses, and foolishly thinks they can do anything (40.6).

The virtue of hope, we see, had it left Pandora's box, would remedy the many maladies and curses. It is very likely that it was kept in the box to allow both fear and despair to plague humanity. If we trust Aquinas, hope is that virtue inspiring us toward our destiny, our goal. However, because hope is for a difficult and arduous good it is often possible to attain through our relations to others. Hope, as I said, is the fundamental awareness that we need others and for Thomas hope is a cause of love (40.7). Later in the Summa, he tells us that the most fitting and absolute other is God (II-II, 17). Unlike Nietzsche, who only thinks of God as a human construct and must necessarily be destroyed, for Thomas, God is real, the proper object of our hope. God is the ultimate personal other who draws us into relationship, into community. He makes captive our captivity.

Finally, Thomas asks if hope facilitates or impedes action and this is critical to empowerment which removes all our bondage. Naturally Thomas sees hope as facilitating action by intensifying our action which is done in two ways. First, it is by virtue of its object as an arduous, possible good stimulating both attentiveness and one's efforts. Second, it enhances our action by virtue of its effects, which cause delight and pleasure (40.7). Hope is that capacity that transforms the shackles in life, lifts up the lowly, removes the oppressive tyrant, that remedies our social evils. Hoping enables the knots to be untied, it allows relationships and connectedness to be restored, and it allows for our common unity to thrive.

Chapter 13

Conclusion: From Suspicion to Trust

The world of ideas, the exchange of ideas, the development of ideas, these make up the atmosphere in which humankind lives and finds meaning. That is why it is critical for us to examine the impact of ideas, how ideas permeate in obvious and in clandestine ways. The *bondage of power* is a twofold dynamic that not only oppresses the other, but the oppressor himself or herself is also oppressed. With the influence of Nietzsche and the other Masters of Suspicion we find ourselves in a climate of mistrust, suspicion, and doubt. Given the extent of Nietzsche's influence, it has been important to see how his ideas have not only given one mastery, but at the same time restricted and limited and alienated. Rather than offering us mastery and superiority over humanity as Nietzsche would claim, we see the dangers of his ideas by widening our scope and posing the question of our connectivity, our interrelatedness.

We are all sojourners in a world of wonder and we must guard against answers that stop us in our tracks. The human mind is restless and ravenous. It is limitless in its capacity to discover. The craft and art of philosophy is not about finding answers, rather it is a romance, a love affair, with the questions that give us the delight of discovery, it is the love of wisdom. We need to get beyond the notion of having the answers. The philosophical task is not knowing, but rather it is the adventure of discovering our ultimate destiny. What we need to understand is this, that, for us to untie the chains of the Nietzschean-Dionysian shackles, discovering our connectedness to what is real, that is the golden key. Consequently, every knot that has tied us is undone when we see the interconnectedness of life. Some critical observations which I wish to summarize from this work, by way of conclusion, where I believe that Nietzsche has failed to see the bigger picture.

First, God exist! Belief in the absolute is essential to human flourishing. Religion and religious traditions bear witness to the conviction that there is a benevolent force at work in the universe (to use the philosophical definition for God). At the very least we must hold that there is a source and sustainer of existence itself which validates the really real. However, as I would tell my students, "The concept of God is a dangerous thing in human hands."

Second, there is absolute truth! Facticity or givenness is real. Our understanding of the truth can be incomplete, but it does not deny the reality of the true. In fact, one of the greatest sources for our interconnectivity is our common pursuit of truth. Agreement and disagreement are essential to understanding what is, as it is. However, without truth, if we say like Nietzsche, there are only perspectives, then my knowledge is opposed to others that do not agree. Or worse, we abandon the pursuit of truth all together, and settle for our packaged version of things. We end up living in disconnected silos, alone, dehumanized. Here we see the lunacy of cultural stupidity – our ideology is more real than the real!

Third, power cannot be owned! To set out to acquire power, physical, or political, is a fool's errand. Power is about potentiality, and once we try to own it, to control it, to limit it, the open-ended possibility is lost. Some power can be used to achieve other positive ends, especially in a mechanical sense. However, once power is used to control others, to force conformity, it becomes treacherous. While morality requires self-restraint, we also see that there is a need to restrain others, but it is always for the common good. For example, when a madman is loose with a gun randomly shooting at people, power must be used and rightly so, but it must be used for the good.

Fourth, human life is an interplay of diverse roles! To fall into thinking that all is reduced to Master-Slave, Victor-Victim, Privileged-Oppressed destroys the vitality of social life. The most important relation we must cherish is found in Martin Buber's notion of the I-Thou.[14] It is an interpersonal, inter-subjective connectivity, the interplay of persons that allows us to engage the other. It requires a maturity that recognizes differences in human relationships which enrich one another and does not exploit. We need one another not because we are the same, but to celebrate the complementarity of our differences. The danger of so-called WOKE thinking is

---

[14] Buber, Martin (1937). *I and Thou*. Translated by Ronald Gregor Smith. Edinburgh: T. & T. Clark.

to reduce persons to a one-sided, one-dimensional characterization. While self-critical thinking is important and we must morally judge our interpersonal behavior, reducing the mystery of human relationships to stagnant labels fails us. We are all engaging in a myriad of interpersonal dynamics that weave our relationships and our friendships.

Fifth, joy is greater than pleasure! The danger in Nietzsche's need to find pleasure in destruction, domination and control is that it never affirms, robbing a person of one's generative character. We find joy in becoming, the bringing into being. Parenthood is the joy of two people bringing forth a new human being. Such generativity establishes a relation of interrelatedness. While pleasure is part of life it can be opposed to life if it is self-serving, hedonistic. Joy is pleasure that draws us into otherness, community, relationship.

Sixth, day is better than night, but we need both! Nietzsche's folly is to see that destruction is the goal. His desire to destroy, to be the antichrist, opts for a greater limitation then he accuses Christianity of denying. Chaos, destruction, endless blaming, is the night with no moon, dark and alone and bleak. It is void of the light. Yet for some aspects of human existence night is better than day, to sleep, to rest from our labors, to see but dimly. Both Light and Dark, Day and Night, Apollinarian and Dionysian are essential, but one without the other is distorted and damaging.

Nietzsche and many thinkers of the last several centuries have put forth a fragmented and compartmentalized world. The Enlightenment turn to the subject, has minimized the importance of intersubjectivity. Disconnection and alienation have been the end result. We see this in our partisan, political world, our constant name-calling, labeling, stereotyping, and enmity, which have made our world and society a place of division. We live in ghettos, creating camps, self-serving enclaves, that enshrine our narrow vision. We are afraid to risk the vulnerability of the other.

Power and its double bondage are the cancer of our day, for it alienates the other, and ultimately oneself. Marx' appreciation of the assembly line's alienating of the work from the worker, applies here as well. In compartmentalizing the creative process into bits and pieces, it destroys the intimate link between the artisan (his or her skills) and the end result (a finished object). The butcher, the baker, the candlestick maker, experience real joy in the end result of their craft, a ham, a loaf of bread, or a candelabra, and then their being drawn into the commerce of the marketplace, that vast arena of interpersonal transaction. The danger of our present Nietzschean climate is alienation and anger, our violent protest, our intolerant ideologies, and our broken relationships. This can only be overcome by a genuine, interpersonal connection and sense of belonging. Hope is the virtue that in our despair, our isolation, our loneliness, compels us to seek the other, to realize that I am not alone and in need of a power outside of myself.

An Epilogue to the Trilogy on Trust.

In all three of these works – *The Tyranny of Perfection* (2020), *The Want of Wealth* (2021), and *The Bondage of Power* (2024) – I have discussed the impact of the so-called "masters of suspicion": Freud, Marx, and Nietzsche. The body of writings from these philosophers have been used to undermine social trust and have detrimentally influenced our political, moral, and religious landscape. For each challenge, I have offered one of the great virtues called theological, or I might say transcendental virtues. **Love** is the virtue that allows for the flawed imperfect in our lives to change, transforming us from ugly ducklings to a new reality allowing us to weave a bond of intimacy with the other. **Faith**, or our ability to believe. changes our greed and avarice to find the real worth in life. And finally **Hope**, our fundamental awareness of our genuine need for the other which loosens the alienating shackles of false power. Each virtue opens us up to a larger encounter with our world. For both Freud and Marx, the virtues of love and faith restore our relation to the world in which we live, and for Nietzsche it is hope that ends the barricade of self-superiority in our risking relationality and vulnerability with the other. So how do we foster trust?

In the May 1999, *Journal of School Leadership* (pp.181-208) – Wayne K. Hoy, and Megan Tschannon Moran studied the question of trust. These authors sought to explore organizational trust in schools, but their findings are illuminating for trust in our social and political life as well. The climate of suspicion is not simply one of questioning and doubt, because such discourse is necessary to building trust. However, a pervasive failure to allow for the goodwill of individuals, a contrarian dismissal of any opposing ideas, is the poison that we see in our political and social world today. Such attitudes fester, giving rise to violence and murderous ideologies. Trust is essential to human flourishing. One of their observations, which shows the impact of trust is: "What are the most consistent findings about people with a trusting disposition is that they are much more likely to be trustworthy than others" (86). Simply put, trust allows for trust. They treat trust as a multifaceted and complex concept. Their insights are a fitting epilogue to *The Trilogy on Trust*.

They also point out that a willingness to risk vulnerability is critical to trust, even preliminary. They observe "Where there is no vulnerability. There is no need for trust" (186–7). To risk, to allow the uncertainty of life and other people, opens one to trusting. Here is the challenge, I would say, that is made real with a sense of love, faith, and hope. Suspicion undermines a society's ability to form community. This bears repeating: **Suspicion undermines a society's ability to form community**. We saw how pleasure, greed, and power created false security, and made risking difficult. The cult of suspicion has become our present challenge. Hoy and Moran declare "Willingness to risk is the degree of confidence one has in a situation of vulnerability" (187).

If we hope to return trust – individual, social, political – we need to learn how to risk vulnerability. Fear, violence, and hatred are some of the greatest obstacles to trust.

So, what might we learn? What might we do to foster trust? Here Hoy and Moran give us a way to foster trust. Trust is a positive quality. They wisely tell us "Trust has a natural attraction. It is good to trust and to be trusted" (186). They identify five facets of trust or faces of trust: benevolence, reliability, competence, honesty, and openness" (186). Allow me to summarize these five faces.

The Face of Benevolence.

For Hoy and Moran benevolence is "the confidence that one's well-being or something one cares about will be protected by the trusted person or group" (187). This shared good will, a sense of our common good, enables us to accept our differences, to allow the other freedom to be, even if it differs one from the other without destroying either.

The Face of Reliability.

Here we see our building relationships that are mutual, ones that share one's self with the other. They observe "Reliability is the extent to which one can count on another to come through with what is needed. Reliability contains a sense of predictability with benevolence" (187). Reliability, unfolds overtime as our relationships mature, and we experience the weaving of lives in a reciprocal sense of care.

The Face of Competence.

Here we see the value of differences and complementarity in our relationships. We see the diversity of gifts and the strength we each bring. When a person demonstrates abilities and skills, we know that they enhance our trust. This competency opens us to a vulnerability as we place our own good and well-being in the hands of another who is capable of caring. “When a person is dependent on another and some level of skill is involved in fulfilling an expectation… [trust is found]” (188).

The Face of Honesty.

Honesty is the critical manifestation of truth. If there is no truth, if we only have individual perspectives, or “private truths” honesty is impossible. My words and my actions must be a genuine disclosure of self so that others may engage. Deception, duplicity, and lies destroy trust. In a world of lies, void of genuineness and integrity, they kill trust. “A correspondence between a person’s statements and deeds characterizes integrity. And acceptance of responsibility for one’s actions, and avoiding distorting the truth in order to shift blame to another characterizes authenticity” (188).

The Face of Openness.

This face of trust "is the extent to which relevant information is not withheld; it is a process by which individuals make themselves vulnerable by sharing information with others" (188). Openness is a kind of gracious hospitality and welcome that draws others into a place of comfort. This character or face opposes the Masters of Suspicion, and its dystopian sense of humanity. "People who are guarded in the information they share provoke suspicions; others wonder what is being hidden and why. Distrust breeds distrust, and people who are unwilling to extend trust through openness end up living in isolating prisons of their own making" (188).

The Tyranny of Perfection, *The Want of Wealth*, and *The Bondage of Power* are a call to explore the voices of mistrust and suspicion we face. To share with others the ideas found in their pages and invite others to engage. But we need to do more, the virtues of love, faith, and hope enable us to courageously confront the weeds and thistles of pleasure, greed, and power. For us to foster trust, to open our society and relationships to trust, we need to risk vulnerability, and to show the many facets and faces of trust: benevolence, reliability, competence, honesty, and openness.

Brief Bibliography

List of Works by Nietzsche & Abbreviations

The Birth of Tragedy (1871)
Early Greek philosophy & other essays (1872)
On the Future of our Educational Institutions (1873)
Thoughts Out of Season (1874)
Human, All Too Human (1875)
The case of Wagner-Nietzsche, Contra Wagner, Selected aphorisms (1876)
The Dawn of Day (1881)
The Joyful Wisdom (1882) [GS]
Thus Spoke Zarathustra (1883)
Beyond Good and Evil (1883) [BGE]
The Genealogy of Morals (1884)
The Will to Power (1885) [WP]
Twilight of the Idols (1886)
The Anti-Christ (1886) [AC]
Ecce Homo (1888) [EH]

Additional Works

Beyond Good and Evil: Prelude to a Philosophy of the Future. Helen Zimmern trans. Willard Huntington Wright intro. New York; The Modern Library Publisher, 1917.

The Antichrist. H.L.Mencken trans. & Introduction. Tribeca Books, 2010.

Walter Kaufman, *The Portable Nietzsche*. Viking Press, 1976.

Mark T. Mitchell, *Power and Purity: The Unholy Marriage that Spawned America's Social Justice Warriors.* Regnery Gateway, 2020

Judith Butler, *The Psychic Life of Power* Stanford University Press, 1997

Michael Foucault, *Ethics: Subjectivity and Truth*. The New Press, 1998

Emmanuel Levinas: *Totality and Infinity: An Essay on Exteriority*, Alphonso Lingis (trans.). Duquesne University Press, 1969.

________. *Time and the Other*. Richard A. Cohen (trans.). Duquesne University Press, 1987

________. *Alterity and Transcendence*. Michael B. Smith (trans.). Columbia University Press, 1999.

________. *Entre Nous: On Thinking-of-the-Other*. Barbara Harshav and Michael B. Smith (trans.). Columbia University Press, 2000.

Friederich Nietzsche *Human, All Too Human: A Book for Free Spirits*. Helen Zimmern trans; J. M. Kennedy intro. T. N. Foulis, 1910.

ACKNOWLEDGEMENTS

Since 2020 when I published the first book in this trilogy, there is even less trust now than four years ago. Most alarming is the amount of institutional mistrust with government and with major media outlets. It would be comical if it weren't so obvious how, across-the-board, these outlets are using an almost verbatim script. These three works*, The Tyranny of Perfection, The Want of Wealth,* and *The Bondage of Power* are timely, and I believe essential to returning trust in our world.

This current book is particularly relevant as the thought of Nietzsche has permeated much of our public life, political discourse, and social networking. Even as early as 1904, four years after Nietzsche's death Jack London's novel *The Sea-Wolf* was a critique against Nietzsche's super-man philosophy.

I have written this book amid my duties as pastor to a growing country parish. When I was sent here, I wrongly thought of a quiet life in the country with ample time to read and write. To the contrary! Post COVID life has been accelerated, and the years of isolation have denied us all the common life so necessary to human flourishing. As we have gone back to being with one another, I find people were discovering the challenge of being with one another. Not an easy task. With our return to social life, it has been going back to work, or to school, or to church where we see that the dynamic of trust has been tested.

In my research and study of Nietzsche, the last of the three so-called "Masters of Suspicion", I could see how pervasive his thought has become. It is a challenging *corpus* to read through and there have been various, even opposing interpreters of his thought. I'm very grateful to my critical readers who came from a wide spectrum, and who helped me clarify my thoughts and my sense of Nietzsche. I would like to thank Fr. Don Goergen, O.P., Joan See, and Rebecca Stephens for their encouragement and help in seeing connections for today. I am also grateful to Ann Garrido, Tollef Graff Hugo, Jeff Vomund, and Anastasia Wendlinder, who each were able to challenge me to greater clarity and appreciation of the cultural complexity of our day. I have maintained a critical reading of Nietzsche, and hopefully I have been fair. His impact on contemporary culture, which is riddled with mistrust, has been interwoven into the failure of contemporary discourse. Any dialogue or discussion today must navigate politically charged phrases, hair-trigger ideological concepts, as well as a sense of self and social alienation in society. These seven readers have helped me to soften some unnecessary harshness and helped me to more sharply focus on the underlying concerns.

Also, I am grateful to Fr. Louis Morrone, OP, my provincial, and Anastasia Wendlinder, my colleague and friend, for their providing encouraging comment to help in marketing this work. Finally, I am thankful for my readers who join me in braving the pages of my books and who, I hope, find the journey a positive and perhaps challenging experience.

DWP

Desert Willow Project

The Desert Willow Project is a pilot program in author independence, fostering greater editorial self-determination and freer creative choices. The project is named for the Desert Willow, a resilient shrub native to the Southwest. It is known for its ability to survive in extreme climates, and still, it blooms with willowy leaves and beautiful flowers, even given difficult circumstances. Not unlike many independent authors, who face extreme challenges, yet their creativity still produces exceptional talent. Opportunities in self-publishing now provide ways for these authors to reach more readers. The DWP promotes the value of independent writers to produce and publish, free from the conventional media industry. DWP authors are also members of the Independent Author Network (IAN), a community of authors who are self-published or published by a small indie press.

DesertWillowProjectUSA@gmail.com

About the Author

Michael Thomas-Paul Demkovich, (1954-) has written on Spirituality, Theology, Thomas Aquinas and Meister Eckhart in journals and books. He holds a Ph.D. and the Pontifical Doctorate, both from the Katholiek Universiteit Leuven. From 1991 to 1996 he taught in St. Louis, MO before becoming the Founding Director of the Dominican Ecclesial Institute (Albuquerque, NM). In 2009 he was named the Gerald Vann Visiting Fellow at Blackfriars, Oxford. He served as President of the International Dominican Foundation and is currently serving in the Archdiocese of Santa Fe as the Episcopal Vicar for Doctrine and Life.

Other Works by this author

"Work as Worth, Money or Meaning" in *Connections Between Spirit and Work in Career Development* (1997)

Introducing Meister Eckhart (2006)

A Soul-Centered Life: Exploring an Animated Spirituality (2010).

The Death of Magister Aycardus (2011)

We Walk by Faith (2018)

The Tyranny of Perfection: Finding True Pleasure (2020)

The Want of Wealth: Discovering Real Worth (2021)

Made in the USA
Columbia, SC
05 August 2024